SIDETRACKS

ALSO BY BEI DAO

POETRY
Endure
The Rose of Time: New & Selected Poems
At the Sky's Edge: Poems 1991–1996
Unlock
Landscape Over Zero
Forms of Distance
Old Snow
The August Sleepwalker
Notes from the City of the Sun

FICTION
Waves

AUTOBIOGRAPHY
City Gate, Open Up

ESSAYS
Blue House
Midnight's Gate

SIDETRACKS
歧路行

—

Bei Dao
北島

—

TRANSLATED FROM THE CHINESE
BY JEFFREY YANG

A New Directions Paperbook Original

Originally published as 《歧路行》 (*qílù xíng*) by Thinker Publishing in Hong Kong in 2022 and by Linking Publishing in Taiwan (台湾联经出版公司) in 2023.

Manufactured in the United States of America
First published as a New Directions Paperbook (NDP1596) in 2024
Design by Eileen Bellamy

Library of Congress Cataloging-in-Publication Data
Names: Beidao, 1949– author. | Yang, Jeffrey, translator.
Title: Sidetracks / Bei Dao ; translated from the Chinese by Jeffrey Yang.
Other titles: Qi lu xing. English
Description: New York, NY : New Directions Publishing Corporation, 2024. |
"A New Directions Paperbook Original."
Identifiers: LCCN 2024004518 | ISBN 9780811238441 (paperback) |
ISBN 9780811238458 (ebook)
Subjects: LCGFT: Poetry.
Classification: LCC PL2892.E525 Q5513 2024
LC record available at https://lccn.loc.gov/2024004518

10 9 8 7 6 5 4 3 2 1

New Directions Books are published for James Laughlin
by New Directions Publishing Corporation
80 Eighth Avenue, New York 10011

ndbooks.com

CONTENTS

For Tianji and Tianhe, the River of Heaven

SIDETRACKS

序曲

為什麼此刻到遠古
歷史逆向而行
為什麼萬物循環
背離時間進程
為什麼古老口信
由石碑傳誦
為什麼帝國衰亡
如大夢初醒
為什麼血流成河
先於紙上談兵
為什麼畫地為牢
以自由之名

難道天外有天
話中有話
電有短路的愛情
難道青春上路
一張張日曆留下
倒退的足印
難道夜的馬群
奔向八方
到天邊暢飲黎明
難道江山變色
紙上長城
也是詩意的蒼龍

誰在聖人的行列中
默默閱讀我們
誰從鎏金的風鈴
從帶血的鞭梢
不斷呼喚我們
誰用謊言的紅罌粟

PROLOGUE

Why does history reverse direction
from this moment to antiquity
Why do the ten thousand things circle away
from the passage of time
Why are the ancient messages
intoned by stone steles
Why is the fall of the empire
like waking from a long dream
Why does the river of blood flow
before the military maps the paper tactics
Why draw prison walls in the dirt
in the name of freedom

Could there be a sky beyond the sky
silent words beneath the words
electricity in short-circuited love
Could youth set out on the road
as page after page of the calendar
leaves footprints going back again
Could the night's team of horses
gallop into the eight directions
and reach the end of the sky to drink up the dawn
Could the changing colors of the rivers and mountains
and a Great Wall on paper
be the Azure Dragon of poetry

Who among the order of sages
is reading us in the quiet stillness
Who ceaselessly calls out to us
from the gilded wind-bells
from the blood-soaked tails of a whip
Who uses the lies of red poppies

照亮蒼茫大地
誰把門窗的對話
賣給穿堂風
誰指揮秋天的樂隊
為小橋迎娶
一盞幽怨的漁燈

哪兒是家園
安放死者的搖籃
哪兒是彼岸
讓詩跨向終點
哪兒是和平
讓日子分配藍天
哪兒是歷史
為說書人備案
哪兒是革命
用風暴彈奏地平線
哪兒是真理
在詞語尋找火山

何時乘東風而來
從沏好的新茶
品味春天的憂傷
何時一聲口哨
為午夜開鎖
滿天星星在咳嗽
何時放飛一隻鴿子
把最大的廣場
縮小成無字印章
何時從關閉的宮門
從歲月裂縫
湧進洪水的光芒

to illuminate the boundless land
Who sold the dialogue between the door
and the window to the cross-draft
Who conducts the orchestra of autumn
to marry the little bridge
and the fishing boat lamp's hidden bitterness

Where is the homeland
to lay a cradle for the dead
Where is the other shore
for poetry to step across the end
Where is the peace
that lets the days distribute blue sky
Where is the history
for storytellers to document and archive
Where is the revolution
that uses a storm to play the horizon
Where is the truth
that looks for a volcano in words

When will you ride over on the East Wind
from freshly brewed tea leaves
taste the melancholy of spring
When will the first tone whistle out
for midnight to unlock
a skyful of coughing stars
When will the pigeons be freed
to shrink the largest public square
into a wordless chop mark
When through the closed palace gates
through the cracks of the months and years
will the bright rays of the flood rush in

第一章

逝去的是大海返回的是泡沫
逝去的是一江春水返回的是空空河床
逝去的是晴空返回的是響箭
逝去的是種子返回的是流水賬
逝去的是樹返回的是柴
逝去的是大火返回的是冰霜
逝去的是古老傳說返回的是謠言
逝去的是飛鳥返回的是詩行
逝去的是星星盛宴返回的是夜的暴政
逝去的是百姓返回的是帝王
逝去的是夢返回的是歌
逝去的是歌返回的是路
逝去的是路返回的是異鄉
逝去的逝去的是無窮的追問
返回的沒有聲響

我是來自彼岸的老漁夫
把風暴的故事收進沉默的網
我是鍛造無形慾望的鐵匠
讓鋼鐵在淬火之痛中更堅強
我是流水線上車衣的女工
用細密的針腳追尋雲中的家鄉
我是煤礦罷工的組織者
釋放黑色詞語中瓦斯的音量
我是看守自己一生的獄卒
讓鑰匙的奔馬穿過鎖孔之光
我是年老眼瞎的圖書館員
傾聽書頁上清風與塵土的冥想
我是住在內心牢籠的君王
當綢緞從織布機還原成晚霞
目送落日在銅鏡中流放

I.

Gone is the sea   the sea-foam returns
Gone is the river of springtime   the empty riverbed returns
Gone is the clear sky   the whistling arrow returns
Gone is the seed   the running tally returns
Gone is the tree   the firewood returns
Gone is the great fire   the hoarfrost returns
Gone is the old legend   the rumors return
Gone is the bird   the lines of the poem return
Gone is the feast of stars   the tyranny of night returns
Gone is the common folk   the emperor returns
Gone is the dream   the song returns
Gone is the song   the road returns
Gone is the road   the foreign land returns
Gone gone is the endless questioning
and what returns has no sound

I am an old fisherman who has come from the other shore
drawing in the story of the storm with a net of silence
I am a blacksmith who forges intangible desires
strengthening the steel with quenched suffering
I am a woman worker on a sewing machine assembly line
using each double stitch to seek a hometown in the clouds
I am an organizer for a coal miners' strike
releasing decibels of gas from black words
I am the jailer who guards over my whole life
letting the key's fleet steed pass through the keyhole of light
I am an old librarian with poor eyes
listening to the meditation of dust and breeze in the leaves
I am a king who lives in an inner cage
and when the loom's silk weave restores the afterglow of clouds
I watch the exile of the setting sun in a bronze mirror

是晨鐘敲響的時候了
是深淵中靈魂浮現的時候了
是季節眨眼的時候了
是花開花落吐出果核的時候了
是蜘蛛網重構邏輯的時候了
是槍殺古老記憶的時候了
是劊子手思念空床的時候了
是星光連接生者與死者的時候了
是女人在廣告上微笑的時候了
是銀行的猛虎出籠的時候了
是石頭雕像走動的時候了
是汽笛尖叫翻轉天空的時候了
是時代匿名的時候了
是詩歌洩露天機的時候了
是時候了

It is time for dawn's bell to ring out
It is time for dead souls to rise out of the abyss
It is time for the seasons to blink
It is time for flowers to bloom flowers to fall and spit out the pits of fruit
It is time for the spiderwebs to reconstruct logic
It is time to shoot down the old memories
It is time for the executioner to crave an empty bed
It is time for starlight to connect the living and the dead
It is time for women to smile sweetly in advertisements
It is time for the banks' tigers to come out of their cages
It is time for stone statues to walk forth
It is time for the steam whistle to shriek and upend the sky
It is time for the Age of Anonymity
It is time for poetry to disclose the will of heaven
It is time

第二章

狂歡是奴隸與百姓的特權
他們用腳投票　　用頭髮興風作浪
歌聲煮沸廣場上的五顆星星
夜與晝在雲中互相追逐
學生罷課　　時針停在午夜時分
垂直的權力上流星飛翔
手風琴展開歲月深深的褶皺
歌手的聲浪滾動石頭也滾動太陽

恐懼與勇敢是同一種子
讓我們的胃隱隱疼痛
瞬息是飛鳥轉向的含義
飛鳥是瞬息持續的形象
兵臨城下必是險招
高山流水盡在手掌中
天空在烏托邦玻璃傾斜
死神握緊年輕的心

半夜　　聽迷霧中的狗叫
死亡的虛線如何抵達終點
紫禁城與交通信號燈
更換的季節卻不可阻擋
打開歷史課本或報紙
埋伏於虎豹豺狼
在漢字的陷阱突圍
地下格柵外也是監獄

革命需要更大的空間
而同一悲劇不可能重演
橫幅標語　　蝨子　　空塑料瓶
吉他手　　傳單　　時針血光
帳篷被大地捆綁的雁群

II.

wild revelry is the privilege of slaves and the common folk
they use their feet to vote   their hair to resist and make waves
songs boil the five stars in the public square
night and day chase each other in the clouds
students boycott classes   clocks stop at midnight
along the vertical axis of power a meteor soars
an accordion opens the deep folds of time
the clamorous waves of the singer roll stones roll sun

fear and courage are the same seed
making our stomachs ache and ache
the moment is defined by a bird turning in midflight
the bird is an image that lasts an instant
soldiers at the city gates must be courting danger
lofty mountains flowing waters end in the palm of a hand
the sky leans against the glass of utopia
the grip of the god of death tightens around youthful hearts

midnight   hear the dogs howl in the thick fog
how can the broken line of death reach the end
Forbidden City and traffic lights
the season of change cannot be stopped
open a history book or a newspaper
ambushed by tiger leopard jackal wolf
break out of the snare of Chinese characters
outside the grate of the underground another prison awaits

the revolution needs a bigger space
so that the same tragedy cannot repeat itself
protest banners   lice   empty plastic bottles
guitar players   leaflets   the glint of blood on the hour hand
the flocks of geese with tents bound to the earth

絕食揮霍最後的口糧
談判與農貿市場　　討價還價
刹車失靈而猛踩油門

救護車流動中響徹全城
林蔭道的樹木蕭立而飢渴
廣場在深夜攝取溫暖
月光浮動　　失眠的人游泳
暴風雨捲走夢的細節
絮語與戒嚴警報激蕩夜空
婚禮在紀念碑旁舉行
藍色探照燈光迎娶新娘

剛刷好的油漆正在褪色
和鏡中的你難以辨認
歷史吃野草　　石頭被移動
北斗七星沒指向出口
利爪夠不到自己的後背
佚名的日記本散落
敘事中更換不同的角色
直到開放的結尾——

所有長夜是詛咒中的期待
所有革命是被背叛的理想
在少女臉上留下淚痕
歷史以外的秘密小徑
引領我們　　狂歡學會悲傷
悲傷中學會默默歌唱
在走出廣場的途中回頭
潮水拍擊夜成為巨浪

hunger strikers squandering their last provisions
negotiations and farmers markets   haggling over prices
brakes fail while flooring the gas

ambulances wail through the city
trees thirst in silence along the shaded avenues
the public square absorbs the heat late into the night
moonlight oscillates   insomniacs swim
the storm whirls away the details of the dreams
whispers and martial law warnings rage against the night sky
a wedding ceremony unfolds beside the monument
the blue beam of a searchlight escorts the bride

freshly brushed paint is already fading
and you have become unrecognizable in the mirror
history eats weeds   stones are displaced
the seven stars of the Dipper point to no exit
sharp claws cannot reach your own back
anonymous diaries disperse
narratives replace different characters
until the end of the opening—

all the long nights are doomed expectations
all revolutions are ideals betrayed
tears run down the face of a young girl
secret little paths outside history
show us the way   to learn how to grieve in revelry
and in grief to learn how to sing silently   silently
on the way out of the square looking back
the tide laps the night into a giant wave

第三章

細節並沒有例外

從河柳抽條到蟬鳴
收起朝代的長卷
路人與來客擦肩掠過
數數城樓的烏鴉
噪音讓人心煩

我的童年我的城市
所有燈火在眨眼

綠色信號彈升起
坦克碾壓唯心歷史觀
地下貝斯斷斷續續
刀鋒划過玻璃
樹根炸裂　　花朵呻吟

口令變成一排士兵
槍是惟一的真理

彈孔裝飾紀念碑
加入自一八四〇年以來
—— 現代史的浮雕
廣場沒打死人
石獅是聾啞證人

從西柏林到北京
佔線　　斷斷續續

這是童謠的北京
不設防的古城
惟有反抗的命運 ——

III.

no exceptions to the particulars

from river-willow strips to cicada song
roll up the long scroll of the dynasty
strangers and guests brush shoulders as they pass
count the crows on the city-gate towers
the noise makes people agitated

my childhood my city
all the lights are blinking

green signal flares rise up
tanks crush historical idealism
underground bass cuts in and out
a knife slices through glass
tree roots rupture   flowers groan

a command becomes a row of soldiers
guns are the only truth

bullet holes decorate the monument
embellishments since the year 1840
—carved reliefs of modern history
"no one was killed on the square"
stone lions deaf-mute witnesses

from West Berlin to Beijing
line busy   cutting in and out

this is the Beijing of nursery rhymes
unfortified defenseless city
the only fate of resistance

讓心握成拳頭
向失敗者們致敬

精靈在電話線呼嘯
是誰　串音或干擾

所有鐘錶停住了
所有煙囪屏住呼吸
所有鏡子轉身
所有騾子蒙上眼
所有水龍頭卡住喉嚨

CNN的突發新聞
正用圖片掃描 ──

城市上空　火光與煙
裝甲車　鋼盔　槍口
血　三輪車　傷員
死亡的臉　人影搖晃
沒有尖叫和槍聲

這是星期日大清早
在故宮筒子河邊

有人照樣吊嗓子
回聲拍擊紅牆
他字正腔圓
唱歪水中的角樓
轟鳴變成低吟
遠征 沒有邊界
鼓點讓歷史過場

向無聲的醫院推進
手術刀停止之處

makes the heart clench into a fist
that salutes the defeated

phantoms screech through the telephone lines
who is it   wiretaps or jammed signals

all the clocks have stopped
all the chimneys hold their breath
all the mirrors turn their backs
all the mules are blindfolded
all the water faucets choke in the throat

CNN breaking news
scanned photos transmitted

the sky above the city   smoke and flames
armored vehicles   steel helmets   gun muzzles
blood   flatbed tricycles   the wounded
dead faces   figures shake
no screaming   no gunfire

early one Sunday morning
at the Forbidden City
by the shore of the Tongzi River

someone still voice-training
echoes bouncing off the red walls
his singing so sonorous and clear
rippling the corner turret aslant in the water
a drumbeat leads history across the stage

pushes toward the silent hospital
at the surgical blade endstation

青春正如古瓷碎裂
自由拆掉舊繃帶
心臟是發瘋的引擎
轟鳴變成低吟
遠征　　沒有邊界

youth shatters like ancient porcelain
freedom tears off the old bandage
the heart is the engine of madness
roars turn into hushed murmurs
military marches   without borders

第四章

西柏林與北京一牆之隔
子彈呼嘯而過　　驚鳥
俯瞰那些吐火的玫瑰

京策爾街五十號四層
客廳的十二吋彩電
北京新聞　　CNN仍在繼續
威士忌　　痛飲生命之水
花白鬍茬繼續生長
溪流在山脊磨亮新月

由一輛廣播車引路
禮拜日下午　　葬禮隊伍
柏林人加入悲愴交響曲
默哀正分開林蔭道
小提琴首席崩斷琴弦

而夏天沒有多遠
雨點 不規則的韻腳
生與死平行在詩中
寫作 —— 那些夜鳥
正從畫框飛出來

顧彬　　疲倦地微笑
戴上憂鬱的面具
在克魯茲堡一起朗誦
空間被回聲所創造
蠟燭　　德文的午夜

一九八二年早春　　頤和園
他用相機對準我
便衣正如我們的影子
而湖光讓人分心

IV.

West Berlin and Beijing divided by a wall
bullets whistle by   frightening the birds
looking down on those fire-spitting roses

Güntzelstrasse 50   fourth floor
12-inch television in the living room
Beijing news   CNN still live
whisky   drink up the water of life
white stubble blooms and blooms
streams on a ridge sharpen the crescent moon

a broadcast news van leads the way
Sunday afternoon   funeral procession
Berliners join the symphony *Pathétique*
a silent tribute divides the avenue
the first-chair violinist breaks a string

while summer isn't far off
raindrops   irregular end rhymes
life and death run parallel through poetry
writing—nocturnal birds
flying out of the frame

Kubin   smiles wearily
puts on a melancholy mask
we read together in Kreuzberg
space composed of echoes
candles   German midnight

early spring 1982   Summer Palace
he pointed a camera at me
the plainclothes were like our shadows
while the lakelight distracted

柏林牆　　地平線藝術節
冷戰僅在想像以外
他獨自到機場接上我
做好麻辣豆腐湯
光的輪子在牆上轉動

悲劇可以替換角色
他把我帶進另一個夏天
我們越過行軍的樹林
公墓　　格林兄弟在那裏

停頓　　某本書的折角
從西柏林飛往西德途中
風敞開雲影的袖口
憤怒　　先知們在播種
更多的加入黑名單

國家電視第二台
新聞時間　　我接受訪談
紅燈跳綠燈　　手勢
女譯者間斷的耳語
聽見空山的回聲

從電話線轉向北京
邵飛說警察們闖進家
他們沒收護照簽證
一股煙味　　像警犬搜尋
玻璃煙缸的灰燼——
那封公開聯名信

三個月後　　哥本哈根
我在市中心的旅館房間
撥到北京的長途電話
我四歲女兒的聲音——
爸爸　　你怎麼不回家

Berlin Wall   Horizon Arts Festival
Cold War exists just beyond the imagination
he came alone to pick me up from the airport
cooked some good spicy tofu soup
wheels of light spinning on the walls

how tragedy can switch roles
Kubin brings me into a different summer
we cross a grove of marching trees
cemetery   there are the Brothers Grimm

standstill   folded corner of a book page
flying en route from West Berlin past West Germany
the wind unfurls the cuffs from the shadows of clouds
wrath   prophets sowing seeds
more names added to the blacklist

state television Channel 2
news hour   I'm being interviewed
red light skips to green   hand signals
broken whispers of the woman translating
listening to the echoes on an empty mountain

lost in the telephone lines to Beijing
Shao Fei said police broke into our house
confiscated passport and visa
scent of cigarette smoke   like a police dog sniffing
ashes in a glass ashtray—
the open letter signed by the thirty-three

three months later   Copenhagen
in a room at a hotel in the city center
I dial long-distance to Beijing
my four-year-old daughter's voice:
Baba   why don't you come home

第五章

屬於河流的兒女們眼神閃亮
原野　　刺眼的陽光磨亮湖面
回憶與子彈共享這世紀
驛車滾動　　直到掌燈時分
囚犯們在月光的同心圓跳舞
懸念的石頭堆積成群山
風暴突擊隊闖入城的記憶

撐緊玩具中生銹的發條
舔過初戀的傷口　　撒點兒鹽
讓兩隻蟋蟀在內心決鬥
果核　　吐下誕生的秘密
在黑板上擦掉彗星的尾巴
貓眼追趕流水的節日
我在旋轉木馬沉思

風車　　攪動多雲的天空
更多的人加入難民的路線
那些不同顏色的語言
來自人類博物館的面具
炊煙在憂傷的黃昏中調色
牧師在燭火的陰影禱告
主用閃電在鞭打城市

噢舊世界的漫遊者
沿着地平線折疊成時間
森林　　呼吸的思想
在陌生小鎮投進郵箱
死亡的陰影在路上飛行
完美的盤子　　手藝
終於脫離事物的本質

V.

the eyes of the daughters and sons of the river are shining
wilderness   dazzling sunlight polishes the surface of the lake
remembrances and bullets share this century
mail trucks tumble along   into the hour of lamplight
prisoners dance in concentric circles of moonlight
anxious stones pile up into mountains
assault troops storm through the gates of the city's memories

tightening the toy's rusted mechanism
licking the wounds of first love   sprinkle a little salt
let the two crickets fight in the innermost heart
fruit pit   spit out the secret of birth
erase the comet tail on the blackboard
the eyes of a cat chase after the festival of flowing water
I ride the wooden horse of a carousel lost in thought

windmills   churn thick clouds in the sky
more people join the refugees' routes
their languages create countless colors
arise from the masks in the museum of humankind
cooking smoke blends the hues of the blue twilight
a priest prays in the shadow of a candle flame
God lashes the city with lightning

O wanderer of the worn world
folded within time along the horizon
forest trees   breathe thoughts
dropped into a mailbox in an unfamiliar town
the shadow of death takes flight on the road
a perfect plate   handcrafted artistry
breaks free at last from the essence of things

醒來　　在小旅館閣樓
窗簾翻飛　　晴轉多雲
油畫的港口　　沒有風帆
城堡下　　人間的喧嘩
被光與旗所包圍
在本地的明信片後面
漢字是第一告密者

向北　　通向孤獨的隘口
深夜的捲尺有多長
測量着可變的氣象圖
情人翻過陽台進入窗戶
桌上　　水果正在成熟
加入失眠者的行列 ——
冬天閃耀的微笑

讓邏輯的手杖開花
禁止繞行麥田的季節
別帶上心事的行李
比衝浪的鎮紙更發狂
歷史如病人的自述
光的步伐在森林穿行
比思路更遠的地方

做夢　　漿果在尖叫
告別鄉愁的盡頭是早晨
找到鑰匙孔的真理

waking up   in the garret of the small hotel
curtains flutter   clear skies turn to clouds
in the oil painting of the harbor   no sails
below the castle   the din of the world
surrounded by light and flags
on the back of a picture postcard
Chinese characters are the first informant

northward   leads to a solitary pass
how long is the tape reel of the deep night
measuring the variable weather maps
lovers climb through the balcony window
on the table   the fruit is ripening
joining the ranks of insomniacs—
winter flashes a smile

let the hand crutch of logic bloom
no detour around the season of wheat
don't bring along the baggage of a disquiet heart
more deranged than a paperweight riding the waves
history like the confessions of a suffering patient
paces of light cross through the forest
to a place more distant than thought

in a dream   berries are screaming
bidding farewell to the end of homesickness is morning
finding the truth of the keyhole

第六章

夜的師傅忙於砌牆
盜火者正加速其心跳
穿過零進入無限
雲中侍者繞過教堂尖頂
所有新聞變成舊雪

奧斯陸　克林肖大學城
和五個小伙子共用廚房
藍色眼睛是多麼無辜
他們偷走我的啤酒
偷走今天的好天氣
而心中熄滅了燈

盲目的夜也成了啞巴
蜷縮在客廳的玻璃窗外
邁平和我一起吃晚飯
他因時差患失語症
關於復刊號的爭論
像冰箱裏的一隻凍雞
復活？還想生蛋孵小雞
沒提到火中的鳳凰
飛鳥掉下一顆罌粟籽

兄弟的影子握緊鑽石
而詞語在歲月逃亡
正是為失敗的意義突圍
無論死者還是新手
讓所有光芒收在書中

下午三點　　太陽落下來
索爾維格之歌引入港口
海水爬上一級級石階

VI.

the master of the night is busy building a wall
the fire thief speeds up his heartbeat
cross through zero and enter the infinite
attendants in the clouds circle the church spire
all news turns into old snow

Oslo   Kringsjå Student Village
sharing a kitchen with five kids
blue eyes so innocent
they steal my beer
steal today's nice weather
and extinguish the inner lamp's flame

the blind night has also turned dumb
huddling outside the glass window of the living room
Maiping and I eat dinner together
he's suffering from jet lag aphasia
we dispute resuming publication of *Today*
—*Revive like a frozen chicken from the freezer?*
while wanting to lay an egg and hatch a chick
no mention of the phoenix in the fire
the flying bird drops a single poppy seed

the shadows of brothers grasp a diamond
while words flee through the months and years
for lost meanings to break through
no matter departed or newly arrived
let all the rays of light be received in the book

three o'clock in the afternoon   sun sets
"Solveig's Song" draws into the harbor
seawater climbs each stone step by step

第一樂句觸動了我
用食指平息波浪的聽眾

哈羅德 一家帶我滑雪
在挪威西部小別墅
雪停了　　我的眼鏡變色
穿過喘息吁吁的森林
壁爐　　風的搖籃曲
北極光激活夢的夜空

一位德國教授請客
自釀啤酒有股肥皂味兒
我和多多一起昏睡
正如雜技的空中飛人
夢裏降落到北京

在學生宿舍看直播
我打開一瓶常溫啤酒
柏林牆　　正翻過世紀
沒有慢動作的日子
不能倒退也不能快進
天外天　　小丑缺席

一九九〇年元旦　　奧斯陸機場
準備飛往斯德哥爾摩
杜博妮、邁平和我喝咖啡
歲末留在咖啡杯底
雪中送別並作出決定

我的拳頭延伸成大錘
在輾轉失眠的鐵砧
推搡的風暴加入鼓風機
星星引爆夜的火藥——

the first musical phrase inspires me to raise
my index finger and quiet the audience of waves

Harald's family takes me skiing
to a small villa in western Norway
it stops snowing   my eyeglasses change color
through the breathless forest   *xu xu   xu xu*
fireplace   wind's lullaby
aurora borealis incites a night sky of dreams

a German professor hosts a dinner
home brew smells like soap
Duo Duo and I both nod into sleep
and with the acrobatic skill of trapeze artists
land in Beijing in a dream

watching the news in the student dorm
I open a bottle of warm beer
Berlin Wall   overturning the century
no such thing as slow-motion days
no way to rewind   no way to fast-forward
sky beyond sky   no sign of a clown

1990 New Year's Day   Oslo Airport
about to fly to Stockholm
Bonnie M., Maiping, and I drink coffee
leave the year's end at the bottom of the cups
farewells in the snow with resolve to resume *Today*

my fist lengthens into a sledgehammer
tosses and turns on the anvil of insomnia
the driving storm expands the bellows
stars ignite the gunpowder night—

第七章

趙一凡攤開手搖搖頭
黃皮書仍在流動中
額頭發亮　　半個世紀過去了
影子是透明的　　騎車
陽光與城市早已褪色

大工棚　　師傅呼嚕聲起伏
調整小燈　　作者已死去
在星空外向我招手 ——
早六點　　高音喇叭
東方紅淹沒建築工地

困惑 我點燃煙卷
沿着使館區的黑色格柵
在卷邊的書遊遍世界
呼吸的春雷比初戀更危險
男孩子們在沙盤推演

九一三事件　　天黑着臉
七十年代沒有結論
滾石停在斜坡上 ——
大錘與小錘　　時代鼓點
思想在鏡子無處躲藏

稻草人是眾鳥之神
煤油燈和心一起跳動
過節　　紅辣椒與爆竹
衣背上汗鹹的世界地圖
鷹爪撕破悲涼的田野

在雙層窗簾的暗室中
被多餘的人所創造

VII.

Zhao Yifan's hands unfold   head shakes
yellow cover books still circulate
forehead shines   half a century passes by
transparent shadows   riding bicycles
sunlight faded with the city long ago

huge tent for the workers   snores rise and fall
adjust the small lamp   the writer is dead
waves to me from the other side of the starry sky—
six in the morning   high-pitched loudspeakers
"The East Is Red" floods the construction site

bewilderment   I light a cigarette
along the black railing in the legation quarter
tour the world in the curled pages of a book
a breath of spring thunder is more dangerous than first love
little boys play soldiers on a sand table

9/13 Lin Biao Incident   day darkens faces
the '70s never ended   a rolling stone
stops halfway down the slope—
big hammer and little hammer   drumbeat of the times
thoughts have nowhere to hide in the mirror

the scarecrow is the god of all birds
kerosene lamp pulses with the heart
celebrate the festival   red chili peppers and firecrackers
back sweat-soaked shirt salt map of the world
eagle claws tear up the desolate fields

in a double-curtained darkroom
imagining the superfluous characters in *Waves*

我承認　　死是其中一章
煙縷在底片過度曝光
搭建成臨時的背景

清明節　　天安門廣場
紙花覆蓋　　以節日的名義
謠言從另一早晨開始
我們一起歌唱父輩的夜
其實早就練習綵排

中央台播音員重播預告
嚴力　　芒克　　和我乾杯
臉部變形　　對視笑了笑
有戲了　　芒克悄悄說 ——
毛澤東逝世那天

他用大手翻翻手稿
這是北京最安全的地方
而第六感官讓我不安
沿命中注定的路線返回
從他手中取走手稿

恐懼　　禮花驀然綻放
探照燈在天花板旋轉
夜的馬達熄滅　　等待天亮
青春是迷途中的囚徒
花盛開也是凋謝

那年冬天　　他被釋放
一滴滴水擊穿黑暗
互相辨認　　無語　　握手
我淚水涔涔
卻不是為了個人的不幸

I concede   death is in one chapter
a wisp of smoke overexposed in the negative
constructs a temporary backdrop

Pure Brightness Festival   Tiananmen Square
covered with paper flowers   in the name of the holiday
rumors from another morning start to spread
we sing to the night of our mothers and fathers
having rehearsed many times before

CCTV broadcast replays the announcement
Yan Li, Mang Ke, and I dry cups
faces change shape   each smile smiles back
There's hope   Mang Ke quietly says—
the day Mao Zedong left this world

Yifan's large hands flip through my manuscript
This is the safest place in Beijing
but a sixth sense made me uneasy
and following fate's path
I returned two days later and took back
the manuscript from him

fear   fireworks suddenly burst into flames
searchlights spin on the ceiling
night's motor dies out   waiting for daybreak
youth is a prisoner of the lost road
flowers bloom and decay

winter that year   Yifan released from prison
a drop of water pierces the darkness
mutual recognition   silent words   handshake
my tears flowed and overflowed
though not for my own misfortune

第八章

公元前四九七年至四八四年，孔子帶弟子周遊
列國十四年。公元前四九三年，他與弟子失
散，在鄭國郭城東門外獨自發呆。

你年近六十
夕陽下　　白髮作筆鋒
歪斜的影子如敗筆
直指東方的故鄉
那些逆光奔跑的孩子
變成象形文字
並逐一練習發聲
破曉放飛一群鴿子
版圖不是為紀念戰爭
你回望炊煙與井

風追趕雲的日子
路牽引驚醒的天空
在山河棋盤上
你與內心的王對弈
閱盡掌中的機緣
一步一步探路
總是敗在自己手中
弟子們已散去
在旗桿上染成暮色
你是惟一的聽眾

吾十有五而志於學
沿禮教的石階而上
你敲鼓擊磬把酒壯行
三十而立　　四十而不惑

VIII.

*From 497 BCE to 484 BCE Confucius led his disciples on a
fourteen-year journey through various states. In 493 BCE,
separated from his disciples, he seated himself alone outside the
east city gate of Zheng and stared into space.*

your years near sixty
setting sun   white hair makes a brush tip
shadow crooked as a flawed brushstroke
points to the homeland east
those children running against the backlight
turn into pictographs
and one by one practice the intonations
dawn sets flight a flock of pigeons
maps aren't for commemorating wars
you turn to gaze at the cooking smoke and the well

days of wind chasing clouds
the road tows awake the open sky
on the mountains-and-rivers chessboard
you play with the king inside the heart
carefully trace the fortune in a palm
step by step explore the path
defeat always at your own hands
disciples have dispersed
dyeing twilight atop a flag post
you are an audience of one

at fifteen devote myself to learning
follow the transmission of the rites
up the stone steps you rap the drums
strike the chimes drink farewell wine
at thirty steadfast   at forty free of doubts

坐而論道縱觀星辰
五十而知天命
從《周易》踏上宦途
穿梭於錦衣華蓋
在空曠的殿堂
你舉杯邀八面來風

六十而耳順
在一生的黃昏時分
你聽到晨光低語的密謀
追隨世代的王侯
宮殿與黃金的燈下沉
回望那起伏的山峰
而你沉迷於音律
三月不知肉味
史書派刺客跟蹤
用多重影子取代你

七十而從心所欲不逾矩
始於足下也會改道
寺廟為了你敲鐘
推開空空四壁
杏壇是虛設的中心
帝王們繞開黃河
群山之首卻毫無幽默
恰有人描述喪家狗
你說得好　趕路前歇腳
城外有多少朝代

sit and discuss the *dao*   survey the stars
at fifty perceive the will of heaven
through the *Changes of Zhou* set foot in court
shuttle forth in brocade clothes to the imperial baldachin
in the vast palace hall emptiness
you raise cups to summon the wind from eight directions

at sixty ears open and willing
during the twilight of your life
you hear dawn light whispering conspiracy
accompanying the aristocracy of the age
the palace sinks with the golden lamps
you look back at the rolling mountains
wholly absorbed with the tuning of the tones
for three months not knowing the taste of meat
history books send assassins on your trail
to replace you with multiple shadows

at seventy do as my heart desires without exceeding the pattern
begin with a single step and still change course
the temple tolls the bell for you
push back the four bare walls
Apricot Altar is the nominal heart
emperors bypass the Yellow River
while supreme Mount Tai is humorless
just as someone once described
that stray dog mourning his lost home
you speak well   stop for a rest before rushing on
the road outside the city through how many dynasties

第九章

冷戰剛剛結束　　飛鳥腹中只有一個太陽　　白帆偏
離了另一條時間的河流　　所有的語言與被奴役的
秩序逆向而行　　我身份可疑　　流亡是穿越虛無的
沒有終點的旅行 —— 我的一生

酗酒 —— 穿過維也納中心的電車搖晃　　在斯德
哥爾摩的住處喝光一瓶威士忌　　我在鏡子扮鬼
臉　　一位南非詩人一位法國詩人和我在奧斯本的
大街上高唱英特納雄納爾　　調整步伐一直踏上原
始的黎明

月亮是我的母親　　輕輕撫平那些秘密的紙條　　突
然想到誕生的痛苦　　正因為生活的殘缺才變得完
整　　父親們的防線成為樹林　　電鋸聲因人類意志
而尖叫　　在墓地後面是閃閃發亮的新城市

落日與二十世紀的輓歌　　散落的編年史和被划掉
的黑名單　　還沒形成的浪頭已經轉世　　戰後的旗
幟不斷變成顏色　　在地下生存的意義汲水　　從
詞語的空隙吐出泡沫　　收集郵票收集思想的碎
片　　蝴蝶翻飛在被遺忘的防線上

我是一九四七年的策蘭　　從布加勒斯特到維也納
穿越邊境　　蛇頭帶着臭鼬的味道　　從童年辨認的
北極星領路　　除了詩稿沒有一紙身份　　在廢棄的
火車站過夜　　星光下彎着腰的影子潛行　　德語才
是母語的敵人　　是石頭開花的時候了

IX.

the Cold War just ended   a lone sun in the belly of the flying bird
white sails drift into an alternate river of time   all languages circulate
against the state of enslavement   my identity suspect   exile is
crossing the void of a journey without a destination—my life

intoxicated—tram gently rocks through the center of Vienna
whisky bottle polished off in a room in Stockholm   I make ghostly
faces in the mirror   a South African poet a French poet and I belt
out "The Internationale" on Osborne Street   adjusting pace to
march straight into first light

the moon is my mother   softly smooth out those secret slips of paper
the birth of suffering flashes to mind   precisely because of life's
incompleteness it completes itself   the defensive line of the fathers
turns into forest   a chainsaw screams out of human will   behind
the cemetery the city glitters and shines

the setting sun and an elegy for the twentieth century   scattered
chronicles and crossed-out blacklists   the wave that has yet to form
has already transmigrated   postwar flags ceaselessly change colors
meanings that survive underground draw water   from the cracks
between words spit out the bubbles   collect postage stamps collect
shards of thought   butterflies flutter above a forgotten line of defense

I am Celan in 1947   crossing the border from Bucharest to Vienna
the smuggler has the smell of a skunk   North Star of my childhood
leads the way   no identity card except a manuscript of poems
overnight at an abandoned train station   a stooped shadow stalks
through the starlight   German the enemy of the mother tongue
it is now time for stone to bloom

我夢見風暴　　森林如發瘋的馬群捲走了我　　摟住
雲中的枕頭　　緊緊擁抱告別的親人　　浪頭拍擊破
舊的木船左側　　苔蘚讓石頭蒙上眼　　在語言的枝
頭上棲息　　戰爭或瘟疫的棺材在飛行　　田野的影
子刨出土豆準備過冬

尋找陌生的城市為了讓我重生　　　烏雲低頭聞到煙
葉的味道　　大海在紙幣留下水印　　　美術館的板
牆上的天使匆匆飛過　　　　廣場的青銅雕像充滿敵
意　　時間就像遛狗那樣撒歡狂奔剎住腳轉彎　　在
樹上蹭癢撒尿繼續向前　　沒有牽引繩

I dream of a raging storm   a forest as if a crazed herd of horses whirls
me away   embrace a pillow in the clouds   hug the family tightly
waves crash against the port side of a battered wooden boat   moss
blindfolds the rocks   perch on the branch of language   coffins
of war or epidemic take flight   shadows in the field dig up potatoes
to prepare for winter

searching for an unfamiliar city in which I can be reborn   crow-
black clouds bow their heads to smell the tobacco leaves   the sea
leaves a watermark on banknotes   angels on the gallery walls fly
away in a hurry   the bronze statue on the public square overflows
with hostility   time is like walking a dog bounding prancing
running wildly swiftly stops and turns the corner   scratches an itch
against a tree then pees and moves on and on   without a leash

第十章

一九八九年八月上旬，陳邁平夫婦開車把我
捎上，早上從紐倫堡出發，傍晚抵達布拉格
市中心。

晚八點　　一組組大小齒輪
緊緊咬合在一起
所有鐘樓正如冬天的心
伏爾塔瓦河解開藍絲絨包袱
理性組裝着國家的記憶
在霧中迷失的街燈走向我
兩個時鐘走得不一致
內心的那個時鐘發瘋似的

卡夫卡是寒鴉
比夜更黑的翅膀在滑行
寫給父親的信已發出
沿着老城廣場逆時針轉圈
櫥窗裏　　玩具騎兵
取代皇帝或父親的王位
女歌手約瑟芬吹着口哨消失
難道老鼠家族追隨風暴

一八八九年　　我出生的房子
毀於大火　　搬到片刻居民樓
三個妹妹出生在這兒
她們在納粹集中營死去
那小行星為我命名
羅馬人把基督釘在天空
導遊為遊客拉開故居的佈景
包括陳邁平夫婦和我

X.

*In early August 1989, Chen Maiping and his wife Anna
Gustafsson Chen were my escorts, picking me up from Nuremberg
in the morning and driving me to Prague where we arrived at
the city center in the evening.*

eight at night   a series of gears big and small
fitted perfectly together
all clock towers are like the heart of winter
the Vltava River unties the blue velvet bundle
reason assembles a nation's memories
the streetlamp lost in the fog walks toward me
two clocks run out of sync
the inner clock looks deranged

Kafka the jackdaw
glides with wings blacker than night
letter written to Father already dispatched
circles the Old Town Square counterclockwise
in a shop window   toy cavalry
usurps the throne of emperor or father
Josephine the singer's whistling fades away
does the mouse family follow the storm

1889   the house of my birth   destroyed by fire
moved into the House at the Minute
three little sisters born here
and die at the Nazi camps
that asteroid 3412 named after me
Romans nailed Christ to the sky
the guide draws open the stage set
of the former residence for the tourists
who include Maiping, Anna, and me

一九八九年　　我們穿越大火
突圍撤退還是逃亡
內與外 —— 東方的智慧
中國長城建造時
權力來自漢字的密碼
石頭建造官僚體系
複製長城複製奧匈帝國
複製太陽城

在主人公K與城堡 之間
向下也是向上的路
帝國與婚姻潛入夜的邏輯
人的孤獨加入狼的共性
墨水瓶中的預言升起
從帽子裏變成信仰
我在父親的背影下咯血
沉默戴上風暴的面具

《手槍評論》並沒有扳機
天鵝絨的大幕徐徐落下
重重人影穿過時代的門框
四年後　　《手槍評論》
邀請《今天》的朋友們
我們在地窖朗誦詩歌
　——從午夜到破曉的鬥爭
消耗了青春的油燈

二○○○年復活節前夕
在老城廣場集市兜售春天
零從空籃子裏變成彩蛋
桑塔格和我一起共進晚餐
紙月亮在風中飄
半夜迷路　　蘇珊轉向我：
沒人再想恢復舊制度
可要的就是這種空白嗎

1989   we pass through the fire
break through the siege to retreat or flee
inside and outside—wisdom of the East
"At the Construction of the Great Wall of China"
power comes from the code of Chinese characters
stones build the bureaucratic system
copy the Great Wall copy the Austro-Hungarian Empire
copy the City of the Sun

between the figure K. and the castle
the way down is also the way up
empire and matrimony slip into the logic of the night
loneliness assumes the aspects of a wolf
prophecies in ink bottles ascend
from a hat and transform into faith
I spit out blood behind my father's shadow
silently put on the mask of the storm

Revolver Revue never had a real trigger
the great Velvet Curtain gradually dropped
one shadow after another crossed the era's doorframe
four years later   *Revolver Revue*
sends an invitation to the friends of *Today*
we read poems in a cellar
—from midnight to dawn struggle on
burning the lamp oil of youth

Easter Eve 2000
peddles springtide at the Old Town Square Market
zeroes in the empty baskets turn into colorful Easter eggs
I have dinner with Susan Sontag
paper moon floats in the wind
lost in the middle of the night   she turns to me:
no one wants to restore the old system
maybe what's needed is exactly this sort of blank space

第十一章

不如相忘於江湖
為了乾涸的源泉

奧斯陸　一九九〇年五月
《今天》永遠是此刻
十個人帶來十面風
十個名字在測量深淵
十個食指觸摸雷電
十個指紋公證的是風暴

狂風吹着詞的裂縫

克林肖學生城
我們為什麼聚在一起
腳步追時針追秒針
軍隊逆轉地球
為某個手勢阻攔風暴
為什麼聚在一起
從風暴眼中出發

盲人領着盲人
在事故和故事之間
在新大陸和舊地圖之間
文學的意義在哪兒
李陀用挪威刀比劃
刀尖戳在桌面上

直到另一個詞的邊界

XI.

better to forget each other in rivers and lakes
when the wellspring has dried

Oslo   May 1990
Today marked "The Moment" forever
10 individuals bring 10 faces of the wind
10 names to measure the abyss
10 forefingers to touch thunder and lightning
10 fingerprints to notarize the storm

as the gale rushes through the cracks in words

Kringsjå Student Village
why do we come together
footsteps chase the hour hand chase the second hand
military troops reverse the spin of the Earth
stop the storm for a gesture
why come together
setting off from the eye of the storm

the blind leading the blind
between plotted accidents and accidental plots
between the New World and old maps
where is the meaning of literature
Li Tuo brandishes a Norwegian knife
jabs the blade tip into the table

plunging straight into the border of another word

遠征 ── 為掙脫身影
問路 ── 尋找家園
閱讀 ── 在鏡中迷失方向
詩歌 ── 為河流送葬
暴君 ── 變成幽靈
歷史 ── 時光即廢墟

為了擰住水龍頭歌唱

高行健的鏡片閃爍
顧左右而言他
那箭頭永遠指向流亡
隱身於詞的林莽
他留下劇本《逃亡》
為復刊號做廣告

打開狼與狼的空間

挪威春天的陽光
照亮古老的小木屋
沿樓梯合影：九個人
迷上深淵的微笑
我們面對着死亡鏡頭
鏡框以外是記憶

鐘聲忽明忽暗

還有叫外號老木的人
他側面低頭走神
聆聽暴風雨的迴響
從天安門廣場的舞台
他拐進巴黎街頭
成為追隨狗的流浪漢

long military march—to break free of the figures
ask directions—to look for home
reading—to lose the way in a mirror
poetry—burial rites for the river
tyrant—turns into a ghost
history—time becomes ruins

to twist off the faucet's singing

Gao Xingjian's lenses flicker
looking left then right words digress
the arrow that forever points toward exile
disappearing in a thicket of words
he left his play *Escape* behind
for the relaunch of the magazine

open a space between wolf and wolf

Norway's spring sunlight
brightens the ancient little log-cabin room
group photo on the staircase: nine people
with smiles possessed by the abyss
as we face the death scene
memory exists outside the frame

the sound of the clock brightens and dims

and there's one nicknamed Old Wood
who bows his head lost in thought
listening to the echoes of the rainstorm
from the platform in Tiananmen Square
he turns onto a street in Paris and becomes
a transient chasing a dog

在奧斯陸中心港灣
從棧橋通向無夢的深處
赤腳舔着甲板的鹽
我們一起喝啤酒
此地也是彼岸
低吟應和傷心的歌

at Oslo's central harbor
following a pier to dreamless depths
barefoot licking the salt from the planks
we drink beer together
here being the other shore too
softly singing echoing a sad song

第十二章

一九七八年北京之秋
命運女神用手語引領我們
無數拳頭搖動西單牆
搖動那苦難的無言之門
烏鴉和文字一起叫喊
回聲來自我們的心

我是混凝土工我是鐵匠
我是地與火的兄弟
為了珊珊的靈魂悲泣
我逆流向死而生
穿過新與舊的波浪的墳頭

狗的鼻子遇上政治
空談季節 —— 為花朵開放
為洗刷無罪的天空
飛鳥吐掉瓜子皮 ——
種子在日夜的裂縫中生長
歷史終於給了我們機會

在那棵老楊樹的蔭庇下
黃銳、芒克和我
半瓶二鍋頭半瓶暗夜
酒精照亮綠色膽汁
為暗夜掌燈共同擊掌
聽太陽穴的鼓手

拉開抽屜 —— 死者活着
影子與影子在決鬥
拉開抽屜 —— 手稿滿天飛
難以辨認他者的身份
當身穿便衣的無名時代
正窺視門後的鎖孔

XII.

1978 autumn in Beijing
the goddess of fate uses sign language to guide us
countless fists pound Xidan Wall
pound on the silent gate of suffering
crows and posted words cry out together
echoes from our hearts

I am a concrete worker I am a blacksmith
I am the brother of earth and fire
weeping for my sister Shan Shan's drowned spirit
I swim upstream toward death to be born
traverse the burial mounds of old and new waves

a dog's nose runs into politics
season of empty talk—for flowers to bloom
to scrub away the innocent sky
birds spit out the hulls from seeds—
seeds sprout between the cracks of day and night
at last history has given us a chance

under the protective shade of an old poplar tree
Huang Rui, Mang Ke, and I
half a bottle of Ergoutou liquor half a bottle of dark night
alcohol illuminates green bile
light the lamps for the dark night clapping all around
while listening to the drumming on the temples

open the drawer—the dead come alive
shadows clash against shadows
open the drawer—pages from a manuscript fly out
the difficulty of recognizing the other
when a nameless age in plain clothes
spies through the keyhole behind the door

沿着一九〇一年的琴鍵　　追上
拉赫瑪尼諾夫的手指
在鐘鼓樓附近的小窩棚
我們正圍着裸燈旋轉
黑膠唱片不斷重放
淹沒一九七八年的文學爭吵
直到太陽在大海中淬火
是的我們一無所有
共同啜飲《羅亭》的淚水
　──　為了自由獻身

沿新街口外大街騎車
在流水中刻下的青春：
我們倆互取筆名
猴子搖身一變──
他是芒克　　我是
被大海浸蝕的島

數數紅綠燈的眼睛
迎來發光的翅膀
幸運的是不幸中書寫
哦天空的讀者──
讓失去記憶的山脈流動
讓鳥路勾勒大地之歌

一張過時的北京地圖
在城鄉結合部某個盲點
冰下是細小骯髒的亮馬河
溫暖的大雪覆蓋此刻──
五個折疊的身影
從油印機翻過一夜

along the keys of a piano 1901   catch up
to Rachmaninoff's fingers
in a small shed near the bell and drum towers
we spin around the naked bulb
vinyl record replays over and over
drowning out the literary feuds of 1978
until the flames of the sun are quenched by the sea
it's true we had nothing
sipping *Rudin*'s tears together
—devoting our lives to freedom

bicycling along Xinjiekou Outer Street
in the youthfulness carved by flowing water:
the two of us chose a pen name for each other
monkey changes form with a wave—
he becomes Mang Ke   I
an island slowly eroded by sea

count the eyes of the traffic lights
welcome the shining wings
fortune is writing in misfortune
O readers of the sky—
let the mountains of lost memories move
let the paths of birds trace the song of the Earth

on an out-of-date map of Beijing
in a blind spot where city and countryside converge
the small and filthy Bright Horse River under the ice
a warm heavy snow covers this moment—
five folded silhouettes
overturn the night through a mimeograph

第十三章

另一個男孩拼世界版圖
語言有另一種顏色
我與影子共飲另一酒杯
和情人一起在另一張床出海
寒流抵達另一港口
我手中放飛另一封信

奧斯陸　　斯德哥爾摩
奧爾胡斯　　哥本哈根
在北歐變幻莫測的天空下
為了尋找另一個太陽
品嘗糖或鹽或砒霜
大雪絮語是暴君的承諾

博魯姆，我的法官
引領我 —— 厄運的影子
在古老的詩歌地圖中
尋找快樂的稻草人
我倆緊緊擠進小電梯
下降　　但沒有地獄

在哥本哈根的法國餐廳
侍者預約另一個日出
打開地下的陽光的紅酒
雪茄好像火車頭
右耳垂的金屬大耳環
夢中　　霧中一閃一閃

是的我睡着了
在桌子或大陸的距離
失眠是永恆的另一向度
鏡中有鄉愁的主人

XIII.

another boy pieces together a map of the world
there is another sort of color to language
I drink another cup of wine with my shadow
with my lover share another bed out to sea
cold currents reach another harbor
my hands let fly another letter

Oslo   Stockholm
Aarhus   Copenhagen
under the ever-shifting Scandinavian skies
looking for another sun
to taste a little sugar or salt or arsenic
the ceaseless chatter of the snow is a tyrant's promises

Poul Borum, my judge
escorts me—misfortune's shadow
who looks for a happy scarecrow
on poetry's ancient map
both of us squeeze tightly into the elevator
descend   but no inferno awaits us

in a French restaurant in Copenhagen
a waiter reserves another sunrise
opens up red-wine sunlight underground
cigars like locomotives
a huge metal earring dangles from Poul's right lobe
twinkling twinkling   through the fog in a dream

yes, I've fallen asleep
at the distance from a desk or the Mainland
insomnia is another measure of eternity
the mirror reflects the master of homesickness

中文 —— 流亡的北極光
公雞練習破曉

沿酒精的高度攀登
閃電通向樹根的祖先
讓木柴陳述貧困的火焰
見證的是毀滅的熱情
在白紙寫下第一行
大雪是罷工的精神領袖

奧爾胡斯是另一個故鄉
命運每天敲我的門
散步　　在那棵樹後轉身
病人們等待太陽升起
在海邊留下一個個空椅子

一九九〇年八月四日
我在藍房子留宿過夜
托馬斯彈奏波羅的海
按着某個黑鍵但沒有聲響
貓頭鷹整夜號叫
遇見另一個夢遊人

新世紀加上另一個早晨
托馬斯帶我採蘑菇
下雨　　他穿過森林領路
用軍用小刀剜蘑菇
有的連忙吐掉：有毒

Chinese—northern lights in exile
a rooster practices breaking dawn

scale the heights of drinking
lightning leads to the ancestors of the tree roots
let firewood declare its impoverished blaze
what is witnessed is the passion of destruction
write the first line on white paper
the snows a spiritual leader on strike

Aarhus is another birthplace
every day fate knocks on my door
take a walk   turn around after that tree
patients wait for the sun to rise
one after another leave empty chairs on the beach

August 4, 1990
I stay overnight at the blue house
Tomas Tranströmer plays the Baltic Sea
the black keys he presses down make no sound
an owl calls through the night
and meets another sleepwalker

the new century adds another morning
Tomas takes me mushrooming
it's raining   he leads the way through the forest
uses a small military knife to scoop out the fruiting fungus
swiftly spits some out: poisonous

第十四章

蟬的北京　四面楚歌
那是舊夢的暴民
風沿着磨刀石的方向
垂柳順從朕的意志
沿中軸線貫穿四九城

從什刹海的後門橋出發
我追趕斷了線的風箏
哨鴿抖開整匹藍天
群山湧向瓦頂的排浪
讓後海淹死太陽
魚群吞噬水下的街燈

幽靈引領漕運的終點
鴉片館　漩渦之夜
一盞盞燈籠迎面而來
太監和丫鬟們漸漸消失
野貓沿着夜拾級而上
五更寒　鐘聲變成晨光
另一個朝代醒來

進入胡同迷宮的中心
我學會蛐蛐的口技
爭其王位　在百花深處
蟋蟀王高歌一曲
我開牙而敗下陣來
在夢中的房頂上奔跑

從黑板上擦掉日子
粉筆末　老師頭髮變白
電鈴聲打斷夢遊人 ——
一排教室與火車頭掛鈎
新的一課是階級鬥爭

XIV.

Beijing of cicadas   Chu songs all around
those mobs of the old dream
wind tracks the course of a whetstone
weeping willows submit to the emperor's will
along the central axis through the four/nine city gates

setting off from Back Gate Bridge in the Ten Temple Seas
I chase after a kite with a snapped line
pigeon tail whistles unfurl the whole bolt of blue sky
mountains surge toward roof-tile waves
let Houhai Lake drown the sun
shoals of fish swallow the underwater streetlights

ghosts guide the way to the end of the canal waterway
opium dens   vortex nights
one by one the lanterns close in
eunuchs and servant girls fade   fade away
feral cats climb the slow steps with the night
fifth nightwatch cold   bell toll turns to dawn light
another dynasty wakes

entering the heart of the hutong labyrinth
I master the art of cricket ventriloquy
vie to be king   in One Hundred Flowers Hidden Deep
the King of the Crickets bursts into song
I bare my teeth but lose the battle
running on rooftops in a dream

erase the date from the blackboard
chalk dust   the teacher's hair turns white
an electric bell interrupts the sleepwalker—
a row of classrooms hitched to a locomotive
the new subject is class struggle

冬夜 —— 母親的棉被
沿針腳是我思路的虛線
沿着紙疊的雁群
起筆從左直到雲的南方
煙囪拐脖抵抗西北風
棉鞋的蟾蜍蹦跳
解凍的是綠色的信號

到節日焰火的對岸去
風卷紅旗的河流
影子在行動　　追上山河
高舉父輩們的火把
追上雷與沉默的拳頭
如手掌天翻地覆

—— 隨時準備着
少先隊面向太陽宣誓
星星敲響軍鼓
我從口吃加入合唱
脊椎拔節般成長
我用橡皮任意地塗改
所有多餘的日子

空行 —— 請等等
上個世紀如隔岸觀火
回放的是折疊時刻 ——
狂風正掙脫門框
閃電的鞭梢抽打鬃毛
輒下是奔流的土地
門牙嘶嘶吐出革命
我腎上腺素急升
戰歌加上抒情的翅膀
這是十七歲的戰爭
用耳朵吹響號角

winter night—mother's quilt
the broken line of my thoughts runs along the stitching
along the paper reams of wild geese
raise a pen on the left to reach the southern clouds
chimneys bend their necks to resist the northwest winds
toads in cotton-padded shoes hop and leap
what has thawed is a green signal

go to the festival fireworks on the other shore
wind sweeps through the river of red flags
shadows move   chase mountains and rivers
lift up the torch of our fathers
chase thunder and silent fists
as if the palm of the hand can overturn heaven and earth

—stand ready
Young Pioneers swear an oath to the sun
stars beat the military drums
I join the chorus with a stutter
my spine grows and lengthens like a stem
I use an eraser to willfully wipe away
all the superfluous days

blank lines—please wait
for the previous century to replay the enfolded moment
as if watching the fires burn across the shore—
the gale breaks free of the doorframe
whips of lightning lash the horsehair
beneath the yoke the rushing land
teeth hiss spit out revolution
my adrenaline spikes
battle songs affixed with lyrical wings
this is the war of age seventeen
using the ears to sound the trumpet

第十五章

一千兩百多年的流水
向東　　長江一號遊輪
追隨杜甫　從重慶到奉節
從後甲板推移群山
夜色低垂　　白帆引領我
油燈引領飢餓的魚群

白帝城碼頭　　一級級石階
登天　　向懸崖承諾
杜甫一家終於落下腳
失眠　　他投下我的身影
我傾聽他詩的心跳

夔門打開紙上激流
艄工如筆站立在浪頭
峽中丈夫絕輕死
濁酒遇上多病之杯
晚風吹來杜甫的白髮
回頭望去　　憶壯遊

七四四年初夏　　洛陽
杜甫李白一見如故
入秋　　高適呼嘯而來
三人醉臥在天空下
暈眩的星雲進入音律
空酒壺　　在群山上

君不見盛世山河改
　　—— 高峽出平湖
皇帝夢淹沒白帝城
請註明長江水位
我沿杜甫記住的小徑
在古城牆腳曬太陽

XV.

more than 1200 years of water flowing
eastward   Yangtze No. 1 cruise ship
chasing Du Fu   from Chongqing to Fengjie
from the afterdeck passing mountains
night falls   the white sail guides me
an oil lamp guides a hungry shoal of fish

Baidi City Wharf   stone step to step
scale to sky   make a promise to a cliff precipice
Du Fu's family settled down at last
can't sleep   he casts my shadow
I listen to the heartbeat of his poetry

Kui Gate opens   torrent floods onto paper
the helmsman stands like a brush on the waves
the young men of the gorge make light of death
cloudy wine brings cups of sickness
night wind carries Du Fu's white hairs
looking back   remembering the grand tour

year 744 early summer   Luoyang
Du Fu and Li Bai fast friends at first sight
into autumn   Gao Shi arrives with the whistling wind
the three poets lie drunk beneath the sky
dazzling nebulae intertwine with the melody
wine pots empty   atop the mountain

can't you see the mountain-and-river changes
of the abundant age—*a smooth lake rises in the towering gorge*
the emperor's dream drowns Baidi City
please note the water level of the Yangtze River
I follow the alleyways that Du Fu remembered
sit in the sun against an ancient city wall

一陣陣狂風何處而來
杜甫一步步登高
在白帝廟高台望長江
七六七年重陽節
我喘息— 他咳嗽
把狂風撕成山河碎片

蕭蕭　　風急　　悲秋　　下
猿嘯　　天高　　渚清　　鳥飛
回　　多病　　登台　　潦倒
沙白　　長江　　濁酒　　滾滾
來　　繁霜　　苦恨　　百年
獨　　新停　　萬里　　作客

那些詞被狂風召回
轉瞬間　　頭顱吐出小草
他腳下踏出平仄路
我聽到他應和的回聲 ——
無邊落木蕭蕭下
不盡長江滾滾來

那溜進暮色的孤狼
喧嘩的瞬間匯成河流
波浪複製波浪
我追趕杜甫的背影 ——

七六八年正月出發
對岸的縴夫　　號子聲聲
幽靈在夜色掌舵
沙鷗沿三峽進曠野
平衡於天地間

blast of wild wind⠀⠀where does it come from
step by step⠀⠀Du Fu climbs the heights⠀⠀gazes out
at the Great River from the high terrace at Baidi Temple
year 767 Chongyang Double Ninth Festival
I gasp for air—he coughs
tears up the wild wind into mountain-and-river fragments

sough sough⠀⠀wind picks up⠀⠀sorrowful autumn⠀⠀below
apes howl⠀⠀sky heights⠀⠀islet clear⠀⠀birds fly
return⠀⠀so many infirmities⠀⠀climb to terrace⠀⠀dejected
sand whiteness⠀⠀Great River⠀⠀cloudy wine⠀⠀rolling rolling
nears⠀⠀heavy frost⠀⠀bitter regrets⠀⠀one hundred years
alone⠀⠀now renounced⠀⠀ten thousand *li*⠀⠀wandering on

those words summoned by the wild wind
in an instant⠀⠀a skull disgorges grass
his feet tramp a flat-oblique toned path—
sough sough no end to the shedding trees
on and on the Great River rolls in

that lone wolf who stole into twilight
in a thunderous instant merges with the river
wave replicates wave
I chase after Du Fu's shadow

year 768 set off on the first moon
boatmen pullers on the far bank⠀⠀boom out in song
an apparition handles the helm in the dark of night
a sand gull skirts the Three Gorges into the wilderness
balanced between heaven and earth

第十六章

塞納河才是流動的盛宴

向里爾克致敬 ——
在羅丹可塑的陰影中
借光向厄運學習
給城堡的女主人寫信
鐘舌在觸摸黃昏
邏各斯 —— 他的一生
在上帝之死的路上

向茨維塔耶娃致敬 ——
追隨永遠的異鄉人
從心中放飛一對白鴿
新世紀　黃昏紀念冊
愛是敵意的時差
追趕着死亡的心跳
風中耕犁　情人的閃電

向巴爾蒙特致敬 ——
暴風雪捲走他的詩頁
在革命第二天早上
太陽歌手挑戰午夜暴君
他保持母語的尊嚴
吻別土地　因貧困而富有
留下白銀時代的手杖

向巴略霍致敬 ——
安第斯山脈的搖籃
為花的暴動而鋃鐺入獄
盾與矛的對抗
自由是憤怒的兄弟
空酒杯斟滿西班牙的血
瘋狂的月亮穿越墓地

XVI.

the Seine is a flowing banquet

bends to Rilke to pay tribute—
in the shadow cast by Rodin
he learns how to live through adversity
writes letters to the princess of the castle
the bell tongue touches dusk
logos—his whole life
on the road to God's death

bends to Tsvetaeva to pay tribute—
she follows an eternal stranger
releases a pair of white doves from the heart
new century   *Evening Album*
love is the time lag of animosity
chasing after death's heartbeat
plough in the wind   lightning of lovers

bends to Balmont to pay tribute—
a snowstorm whirls away the pages of his poems
in the morning after the revolution
the sun singer challenges the midnight tyrant
he preserves the dignity of the mother tongue
kisses the earth goodbye   being impoverished yet rich
leaves behind the crutch of the silver age

bends to Vallejo to pay tribute—
cradle of the Andes
shackled and jailed for the insurrection of flowers
a battle between shield and spear
freedom is the brother of rage
an empty wine glass filled with the blood of Spain
a crazed moon cuts across a cemetery

向策蘭致敬 ——
他吹滅漫天的星星
手藝人釋放詞的火花
品嘗母親的杏仁
燈光在不同的窗戶折射
讓鑰匙打開心的位置
米拉波橋刻下流水

向布萊頓巴赫致敬 ——
他的書釣我上鈎
我跟着他的影子逃跑
交叉重疊又分離
清晨　　盧森堡公園
他光腳轉着圈小跑
為永恆的牆哭泣

向達爾維什致敬 ——
來自巴勒斯坦的情人
子彈追上鳥的隱喻
詩歌與坦克對話
故鄉是夢遊的驛站
他的手支撐命運
野花共享血腥的春天

向阿多尼斯致敬 ——
他從赤貧的地平線
到中國南方的桂花香
永恆 —— 火與火的深淵
詩歌是危險的橋
在父親的蘇菲血液中
他撕掉天上的封條

bends to Celan to pay tribute—
he blows out the stars in the skies
the craftsman unleashing sparks from words
savors the almonds of Mother
light refracts from different windows
let the key open a site for the heart
Le Pont Mirabeau carves the flowing water

bends to Breytenbach to pay tribute—
his book of terror hooks into me
I flee with his shadow
crossings overlap and then separate
early morning   Luxembourg Gardens
he jogs in circles with bare feet
weeping for the eternal prison walls

bends to Darwish to pay tribute—
a lover from Palestine
bullets catch up with the metaphors of birds
poetry talks with the tanks
a homeland is the relay station for sleepwalkers
his hands brace fate
wildflowers share the springtide of blood

bends to Adonis to pay tribute—
from the impoverished horizon he reaches
the sweet scent of osmanthus in southern China
eternity—the abyss of fire and fire
poetry is a dangerous bridge
in the Sufi blood of his father
he tears off the seal from the heavens

第十七章

反抗流亡反抗土地的邀請
醒來 —— 太陽的靶標
我的心是世界盡頭的鬧鐘
反抗命運反抗我的河床
加速旋風　　從樹的意志
從無邊野草到重唱的山巒
反抗死亡反抗命運開關
切開蘋果切開時間的內核
記憶　　從空巢到空巢
反抗知識反抗輕的塵土
月光的舞者消失在樹林中
旋風中　　金錢叮噹響
反抗皇權反抗思想人質
影子隊伍追上權力的光源
麻雀腳印在白紙上

推開並隨手關上門
陌生人和我在這條路上
沿着車轍走向他鄉
從翻騰的行雲汲取墨水
誰打開時間之書
愛情播下死亡的種子
當新月拉開滿弓
狂風彈撥無主的琴弦
內心是盲人的地圖
有人在夜留下刻度
鑰匙與鎖是敵對的同謀

秋天的　　小提琴　　嗚咽悠長
怠倦　而單調　刺傷我的心
諾曼底 —— 無名的沙灘
青春的血　　翅膀與天空

XVII.

Resist exile resist earth's invitation
rising awake—target of sun
my heart the alarm clock at the edge of the world
Resist fate resist my riverbed
quicken the whirlwind   through the will of the trees
through the boundless wild weeds to the chorus of mountains
Resist death resist the power switch of fate
cut open an apple cut out the kernel of time
memory   from empty nest to empty nest
Resist knowledge resist the gentle dust
a moonlight dancer disappears into the forest
in the whirlwind   money clinks clinks cha-ching
Resist imperial authority resist hostages of the mind
an army of shadows engulfs the light source of power
sparrow tracks on white paper

push open and then shut the door
a stranger and I walk this track
follow the wheel ruts to a foreign country
draw the ink from churning clouds
who opens the book of time
love sows seeds of death
when the crescent moon pulls a full bow
the gale plucks the strings without a master
the heart is a map for the blind
someone leaves hatch marks in the night
lock and key are enemy conspirators

of autumn   violins   sobs prolong
languorous   and monotonous   prongs my heart
Normandy—nameless beach
blood of youth   wings and sky

那是最漫長的一天
很多年過去了　　音樂
留下樂譜中完美的形式
退潮　　留下空白的意義
歷史的僕役隱退　　繼續前進
追上一連串懷舊的日子
追上手挽手的浪花
追上一顆子彈離別的意義
追上歷史以外的足音

新雨在逆向車燈穿行
吹響號角　　到天邊
樹冠如頭髮那樣變色
那是嘆息的國度
跟隨父親們的背影
水平線收進夜的折刀
琴弦斷了　　曲終戛然而止
桌子才是真實的邊界
而工作斷斷續續
背後是隱秘的冬天
雲的思想成為一顆流星
照亮那大地的瞬間 ——
兵書落雪　　漢字圍城

that day the most endless of days
so many years have gone   music
leaves behind the score's perfected forms
ebb tide   leaves blank meanings
the servants of history retire   and continue on
chase a string of nostalgic days
chase the hand-in-hand spray of the waves
chase the meaning of a bullet's departure
chase the sound of footsteps outside history

fresh rain passes through the car's reversing lights
blow the horn   reach the end of sky
tree crowns change colors like hair
that's the nation of sighs
following the shadows of the fathers
waterline takes in the night's folding knife
string breaks   song cuts off
the desk is the real border
and work comes and goes
the secret winter in the background
a cloud's thoughts turn into a shooting star
that illuminates the earth's moment—
snow falls from the book of war   besieged
fortress of Chinese characters

第十八章

讓人類加入星雲般暈眩的時刻　　我找到一份檔
案分類的臨時工作　　敲打着接近複調音樂的鍵
盤　　吞咽的是現實三明治　　追上一寸一寸的真
理——

生於一九二六年六月三日　　我和宇宙一起誕
生　　在生銹的排水溝格柵也是同一扇上帝的天
窗　　父親的背影像雨燕迅速消失在閃電中　　校
車的車燈穿越母親向左瘋狂的深淵

老虎! 老虎! 你金碧輝煌，火似地照亮黑夜的林莽
小手風琴和古老的肺那樣舒展　　爵士樂淒厲的
小號在風中穿行　　記憶之刃犁開惠特曼的田野

艾倫是我的攝影師傅　　相機鏡頭是死亡的大師
從夜的膠卷沖洗到鏡框的天空　　他教我在首爾
市中心的路邊打坐　　我問起轉世　　一隻在枝
頭的烏鴉飛起

蓄着大鬍子裝扮成獅子引導叢林的意義　　造反
加詩歌是不倦的火車頭　　讓黑山派的呼吸法召
喚翻天覆地的暴風雨　　在喇嘛教練習手印與禪
坐中冥想　　毒蘑菇是欲仙欲死的微型原子彈

我們內心都是美麗的金色向日葵，　　我們獲得自
己種子的祝福　　跨越母親的黎明的界河　　在死
亡之路打聽另一個季節　　禿鷲盤旋在西藏高原
的金頂之上

XVIII.

let humanity join the nebular whirl of the times   I've found a
temporary job classifying records   tapping on the keyboard ap-
proaches polyphonous music   swallowing a *reality sandwich*
catching up with the truth inch by inch—

born in 1926 on the third of June   I came into being with the
universe   a rusted gutter grate was also God's skylight   Father's
shadow vanishes like a swift in a flash of lightning   the headlights
of a school bus pass left of the abyss of mother's madness

*Tyger! Tyger! Your gold jade brightness, firelike lights up the lush
forests of the night*   the bandoneon stretches out like an
ancient lung   mournful jazz trumpet solo threads through the
wind   the blade of memory plows Whitman's open fields

Allen is my photography shifu   the camera lens is the master of
death   from the night's developing film to the framed sky   he
teaches me to meditate sitting on a sidewalk in downtown Seoul
I ask about reincarnation   a crow on a branch takes flight

the meaning of growing a giant beard to disguise oneself as a lion
guiding the jungle   revolt gives poetry an inexhaustible loco-
motive   let Black Mountain School pranayamas summon the
tempest that overturns heaven and earth   practice Tibetan Bud-
dhist mudras and tantric meditation   magic mushrooms are
tiny atom bombs of death-wish transcendence

*our hearts are beautiful golden sunflowers, we all receive the bless-
ings of our own seed*   leaping across Mother's dawn river border
ask about another season on the road to death   vultures spiral
above the golden roof of the Tibetan Plateau

艾倫死了　中國清明節的週年祭日　我穿過時
代廣場沿十四街拐到第三大道　從沸騰的廣場
到流動的小街　合上群山憤怒與大海呼吸的書

Allen has died   on the Chinese festival day of Pure Brightness
I pass through Times Square down to 14th Street and turn to-
ward Third Avenue   from boiling public square to flowing
cross streets   close the book of the raging mountains and the
breathing seas

第十九章

一九三六年夏　　一陣槍聲
一群野鴿驚飛　　掙脫大地
兩個鬥牛士一個教師和
洛爾迦　在格林納達山腳下
橄欖樹林旁 —— 空彈殼
歷史在天空打字

一九九二年冬　　一路開車
往南　　我們奔向格林納達
深歌追尋流浪的搖籃
弗拉明戈穿上火焰
按死亡的節奏擊掌而歌
阿爾罕布拉宮的回憶
沿着時光迴廊　　循環流動
石柱後遇見洛爾迦

一九三三年春　　西班牙
戴望舒　練習語法的小路
在市鎮廣場和小酒店
到處是歌謠與愛情
風暴的侍者鋪開地平線
掀起桌布　　麵包屑 ——
跨邊界的中文飛翔

一九七一年　《洛爾迦詩鈔》
一雙手傳遞另一雙手
呼吸轉向呼吸 —— 屏息
字與字之間 —— 腳下都是深淵
跑書　跑　書的地平線
自行車穿過胡同與字裏行間
車鈴搖響秘密的天空
頭髮染上洛爾迦的綠色

XIX.

summer 1936   a burst of gunfire   a flock
of rock doves takes off   struggles free of the earth
two bullfighters one teacher and
Lorca   at the foot of the mountains of Granada
by the olive tree groves—empty bullet shells
history types on the sky

winter 1992   driving on a road
south   we head for Granada
deep song pursues the cradle of vagrancy
flamenco dresses with flames
restrains the clapping rhythm of death in song
Alhambra palace memories
along the covered corridors of time   move in a circle
bump into Lorca behind a stone pillar

spring 1933   Spain
Dai Wangshu   practices grammar on the little streets
from the public squares to the village tabernas
everywhere folksongs and romance can be found
the waiter of the storm spreads out the horizon
lifts the tablecloth   breadcrumbs—
Chinese soars across the border

1971   *Lorca: Selected Poems*
passes from a pair of hands to another pair of hands
breath to breath—breathless
word to word—the abyss stretches underfoot
runs the book   runs   the horizon of the book
pedaling through hutong alleys and the words between lines
bicycle bell rings out the secret sky
hair dyed Lorca green

直到七十年代　　洛爾迦
你屬於北京的地下沙龍
隱身煙霧　　喝下月光
—— 群星中的無冕之王
你被捲入地下詩人的爭吵
警察嗅聞可疑的筆跡
為了女人打群架
—— 新月與落日的決鬥

二〇一一年五月　　從奧爾維拉
到馬德里　　我在寄宿學院朗誦
當大鋼琴浮出水面
洛爾迦的手指彈奏流水
大廳傾聽世紀的回聲
在勞拉‡ 的基金會辦公室
我觸摸他的鉛筆手稿 ——
燃燒的影子在雪上滑行

今晚　　燕保羅約我相聚
穿過法國大使館官邸
在本地小餐館就坐
燭火搖曳　　讓銀河放電
照亮馬德里保衛戰
國際縱隊也包括中國人
車輪四季閒置　　市長的兒子
在流亡中誕生長大
並非為風暴中的祖先哭泣

through the 1970s   Lorca
you belong to a Beijing underground salon
hidden smokes   swigging moonshine
—the uncrowned king of the stars
you are drawn into the quarrels of underground poets
police sniff suspicious handwriting
fights break out over girls
—the crescent moon duels the setting sun

May 2011   I leave Olvera
for Madrid   to read at the Residencia de Estudiantes
where a grand piano surfaces on the water
Lorca's fingers play the flowing waters
the hall listening to the century's echoes
in Laura García's office at the foundation
I touch his manuscript handwritten in lead—
burning shadows slide on the snow

now evening   Paul Jean-Ortiz has asked me to meet
pass through the French ambassador's residence
take a seat at a small local restaurant
candle flames flicker   make the Silver River galaxy discharge
electricity   lights up the defense of Madrid
Chinese volunteers also in the International Brigades
wheels idle for four seasons   the mayor's son
born and raised in exile
doesn't weep for the ancestors in the storm

第二十章

生活是多麼緩慢
希望是多麼暴力
暴力在尋找新的河床
喚醒拳頭　　擂動我的生活
登高的人粉刷藍天
鐘舌搖動　　喚醒沉寂的心
巴黎我的第二故鄉

一九八九年初夏　　巴黎
燕保羅和愛麗絲的成員
黃雀行動的終點
保羅和呂敏面對面
在午夜的國境線
移動那些星星的棋子
破曉 —— 在停機坪着陸
迎來神秘的客人

法國難民　　我炫耀的烙印
威尼斯街七號　　我打開窗戶
時光倒流而寓言向前
所有屋瓦為暴風雨鼓掌
從圍城漢字到放射形廣場
記住了丁香的呼吸

我是高源　　老子就是我
我和歷史開個玩笑
圍棋 —— 山河就在我腳下
數數黑子和白子
黑夜永遠比白晝長

高源朝我連打了兩個噴嚏
從病毒到宇宙的邊界

XX.

how slow life moves
how violent hope proves
violence searches for a new riverbed
awakening fists   that pound my life
those high above whitewash the sky
the bell tongue swings   awakening the silent heart
Paris my second home

early summer 1989   Paris
Paul Jean-Ortiz and a member of ALICE
the final stop of Operation Yellowbird
Paul and Lü Min face each other
at the border of midnight
moving those chess pieces of the stars
daybreak—landing on the tarmac
welcomes the mysterious guests

a refugee in France   I flaunt the brand
7 rue de Venise   I open the windows
time reverses and an allegory proceeds
all the roof tiles applaud the tempest
from the besieged fortress of Chinese characters
to the radial Place de l'Étoile
remembering the breath of lilacs

I am Gao Yuan   and Lao Zi is me
I joke around with history
game of Go—mountains and rivers at my feet
count the black stones and white stones
the darkness of night is always longer than the light of day

Gao Yuan sneezes twice in a row at me
from a virus to the boundary of the universe

夢回他鄉　照片上的刑場
夜落下永別的閘門
而成都口音是法文遠親
最新的中文報紙蓋住他的臉
夢見瘸腿的歷史走來

我是老木　沒人認識我
我拽長一根地平線
去羅馬我度過了一生
我不在乎國王還是流浪漢
向太陽牽着的狗致敬

往事從地鐵出口浮現
浪頭昂首　拍擊無形的礁石
我看到老木的背影
歲月呼嘯而縮小成句號 ——
在北京多雪的二月
一封公開信折疊成紙飛鏢
消失在陌生人的森林中

我是宋琳　而鏡子是空的
背後是一條河的家族史
洞簫吹起　天在詩以外
狂風在我的脊椎試音

斜坡確認我們詩的位置
在某個街角的咖啡館
鑄造頭顱　水銀流動的手
觸摸薊與彼岸的話題
夜在杯底　打開一把把傘
對峙的意義　我說
我們沿着塞納河邊散步

dreaming of returning to a foreign land   in a photograph
an execution ground   night falls
on the gate of eternal farewell
Chengdu accent distantly related to French
a fresh Chinese newspaper covers his face
crippled history walks over in a dream

I am Lao Mu   no one knows me
I drag the long line of the horizon out
to Rome where I pass a lifetime
I don't care if kings or transients
salute the dogs led by the sun

events from the past float out of a subway exit
waves curl up   crash against a formless reef
I see Lao Mu's shape from behind
the years screech and shrink into a period—
in a snowy Beijing February
an open letter folds into a paper dart
and vanishes in a forest of strangers

I am Song Lin   and the mirror is empty
the background is a river of family history
notes from a xiao flute out   heaven is beyond poetry
wild winds test the tones of my vertebrae

the slope confirms the place of our poetry
at a certain street corner café
cast metal skulls   hands of liquid mercury
talk touches on tiger thistle and the other shore
night at the bottom of a cup   opening umbrellas
the meaning of confrontation   I say
we stroll along the banks of the Seine

第二十一章

我是零號病人
從小瓶子放出的幽靈
戴上花冠　　我君臨天下
所有權力跪在地上
被訓誡的鏡子關閉門窗
道路繞開封城的法令
而追逐心跳的鐘錶停擺 ——
自由失去自由
時間告別時間

我是零號病人
在上帝命名萬物以前
誰指揮地貌變遷的交響樂
響箭　　多餘的日子
穿過野史和砍伐的森林
紅狐尾巴在帝國的廢墟跳躍
我是零 —— 吹響口哨
我為陌生人親吻
姓名獲得石頭的重量

我是零號病人
李文亮醫生發現了我
在電腦屏幕互相辨認
生與死　　晝與夜　　漩渦
從水下吐出一串串泡沫
李醫生戴氧氣罩 ——
真相比平反更重要
沿走廊盡頭　　我貼近你
在黎明前吹滅油燈

我是零號病人
陰影是太陽的領路人

XXI.

I am patient zero
a spirit released from a tiny bottle
donning a flower crown   I reign over the world
all the powers that be kneel before me
the admonished mirror closes the doors and windows
the road bypasses the citywide lockdown
and the clock that chases the heartbeat stops—
freedom loses freedom
time bids farewell to time

I am patient zero
before God named the ten thousand things
who conducted the symphony of the earth-changing landscape
whistling arrows   superfluous days
passing through unofficial histories and felled forests
a red fox tail bounding among the ruins of empire
I am zero—let loose a loud whistle
I kiss strangers
names gain the weight of stone

I am patient zero
Dr. Li Wenliang found me
ID'ing each other on a computer screen
life and death   day and night   whirlpool
spit out a string of bubbles underwater
Dr. Li wears an oxygen mask—
the truth is more important than vindication
to the end of the passageway   I press close to you
blow out the oil lamp before dawn

I am patient zero
a shadow is the sun's guide

失憶的廣場　　邏輯的小巷
沒有門　　也沒有鑰匙
所有記憶的釘子
正加固人類的苦難
很多年　　潛伏在冰河時代
時間與戰馬呼嘯而過
我終於倖存下來

我是零號病人
在數字星空與大海之間
在活火山與凍原之間
在恐龍與外星人之間
在語言之路與鐵柵欄之間
我被自由所包圍
以國家的名義判處極刑
被科學家們追殺
我無罪 —— 萬物瘋狂生長

我是零號病人
被放逐而逆流而上
不投河 —— 我沒有祖國
腳下是轉世的深淵
書　　為練習飛翔
而謊言的太陽照樣升起
我的傷口閉上眼睛
在動物啜飲的瓦罐中
溢出母愛的睡眠

public square of amnesia   alley of logic
no door   and no key
all the nails of memory
reinforce the suffering of humanity
so many years   hidden in the ice age
time   and war horses   roar by
in the end I survived

I am patient zero
between the sky of digital stars and the sea
between the active volcano and the tundra
between the dinosaurs and the extraterrestrials
between the path of language and the iron fence
I am besieged by freedom
sentenced to execution in the name of the nation
hunted down by scientists
I am innocent—whatever exists grows like crazy

I am patient zero
banished   swimming against the current
without drowning in the river—I have no motherland
underfoot is the abyss of reincarnation
books   for practicing how to fly
while the sun of lies still rises
my open wounds shut their eyes
where animals sip from earthen jars
spilling over with the sleep of a mother's love

第二十二章

繼續向前　　生活被刪節
口罩　　影子在呼吸　　而飛鳥
進入公共事件　　敞開光芒
空城與冥想　　號角呼喚
落日　　命與運短路　　導火索 ——
被打發的口信呼嘯　　讓語言
打開牢籠　　讓多情的種子
在姻緣的縫隙開花　　病毒
屬於開拓的黑暗國度

希臘如夢　　歷史以外是
大海 —— 墨水在天空書寫
諸神冬眠　　向沉默的島嶼撒網
伯羅奔尼撒　　盲詩人荷馬
馬蹄踏歌　　為道路命名
古劇場　　在舞台中心歌唱
天空盤旋　　烏鴉觀眾一起消失
花吐出種子 —— 正午思想
加繆　　合上日記是墓碑

地中海的天堂 —— 馬略卡島
蕭邦和喬治·桑　　為了過冬
陽光醫生　　從肺結核查到夜
修道院的狗向世紀狂吠
正如兩個輕騎兵　　在鍵盤跳躍
紙上足跡　　跨越誓言的橋
在光的柵欄突圍　　拉響汽笛
乘小火車出發　　從帕爾馬
到索列爾港　　燈塔不再守望大海

馬拉喀什　　王國的迷宮
權力隱身於露天市場　　野蠻人

XXII.

keep moving   life abridged
masks   shadows breathe   and flying birds
join the public sphere   unrestricted rays of light
city empty meditation   horns blare out
setting sun   life short-circuited fate   burning fuse—
sent messages howl   let language
open the cage   let seeds of amorous affection
bloom in the cracks of marriage   virus
belongs to the dark nation of exploitation

Greece like a dream   beyond history is
the sea—ink written in the sky
the gods hibernate   throw a net toward the silent island
Peloponnese   the blind poet Homer
horse hooves stamp a song   naming the road
ancient theater   sing at the center of the stage
sky spirals out   audience of crows disappears as one
flowers spit out seeds—noon thoughts
Camus   shut diary is a gravestone

Mediterranean paradise—Mallorca island
Chopin and Sand   passed the winter here
sunshine doctor   from tuberculosis tests into the night
dogs at a monastery bark wildly at the century
like two light cavalry   jumping on the keyboard
footprints on paper   cross the bridge of promises
break out of the enclosure of light   pull the steam whistle
set out in the little train   from Palma
to Port de Sóller   the lighthouse no longer guards the sea

Marrakech   labyrinth of the kingdom
power hides in the open-air marketplace   *barbari*

等待上帝　　男孩子們叫喊
—— Corona, China
屠宰場與皮革業　　向黎明祈禱
井吞吐太陽　　小巷織成網
賊追新月　　駱駝牽着遠山
漂泊故我在　　為了尋找
路標 —— 糾正偏離的歷程

洛杉磯的狼群追趕音樂
從新大陸第二章到北京童謠
帶條紋的老虎穿過火環
回到二〇二〇年春天
施耐德 —— 九十歲生日
我們通電話　　山谷幽深
森林裏留下野兔的足印
光織成山河　　火餵養黑夜
他和鹿一起攀登 在群峰之上 ——

戴維斯　　心如困獸
我在畫畫　　從此刻到天涯
在雲中行走　　汲水
廚房面對田野　　陽光桌布
刀叉閃電　　與往事乾杯
一輛救護車穿過起伏的麥浪
突然敲門　　庚子驟然轉身
用真相佔領夢的空間
醒來　　仍在隔離中

waiting for God   boys yelp out
—*Corona! China!*
abattoir and leather workshop   face the dawn to pray
a well swallows and spits out the sun
the small alleyways weave a net   thieves pursue
the crescent moon   camels pull the distant mountains
wandering, therefore I exist   so as to search for
road signs—correct the deviated course

the wolf pack of Los Angeles chase the music
from Dvořák's "New World" second movement
to Beijing nursery rhymes   the striped tiger
leaps through the ring of fire
returns to the spring of 2020
Snyder—ninetieth birthday
we talk on the phone   deep valley silence
wild rabbit tracks in the forest
light weaves mountains and rivers   fire feeds the night
he and a deer climb together   above the peaks—

Davis, CA   heart like a trapped beast
I paint pictures   from this moment to the end of sky
walk in the clouds   draw water from the well
kitchen faces fields   sunshine tablecloth
knife fork lightning   drink to the past
an ambulance crosses rippling waves of wheat
rapid knocks on the door   metal rat year abruptly turns
occupy the space of a dream with the truth
waking up   still in isolation

第二十三章

洋葱剝皮　　胡椒和現實被粉碎
火雞放進烤箱　　定時加溫
一九九四年十一月二十四日　　感恩節
離開舊金山　穿過子午線
北京首都機場　　我跟上歲月排隊
邊檢小窗　　戴軍帽的月亮
鄉愁 —— 插頭接上電源
而互聯網鎖住了我的名字
我的秘密花園　　沒收詩的種子

秘密的客人們終於來了
逼着我說出我的名字
是我　　被激怒祖先的鏈條
和山巒　　拒絕回答所有的質問
錄像機和錄音機對準我
筆錄供詞　　一張飢餓的白紙
夜幕拉開我的獨幕劇
我洗碗筷　　板牆後是草地
太陽像死囚等待死刑

張上校　　生鏽的笑容
齒輪咬緊　　為攀登他的一生
而嘴角露出人性的瞬間
我是劇中主角　　裸燈
與漩渦的夜周旋　　我夢遊 ——
讓存在的時間吐絲
自縛的繭比宇宙更可靠
我的名字引領另一個名字
舞台轉動　　我追趕着我

獨白：在漢字中越獄
人影投向天幕　　重重疊疊

XXIII.

peel the onions   pepper crushed with reality
place the turkey in the oven   time set temperature
November 24, 1994   Thanksgiving Day
depart from San Francisco   cross the prime meridian
Bejing Capital Airport   I line up behind the years
little window of immigration   the moon dons a military cap
homesickness—electric plug connects to a power source
and the internet locks my name
my secret garden   confiscated seeds of poetry

the covert guests finally arrive
force me to utter my other name
it is I   a chain of enraged ancestors
and the mountains   refuse to answer any questions
video recorder and tape recorder aimed at me
written confession   a starving blank sheet of paper
the curtain of night opens my one-act play
I wash chopsticks dishes   behind the wood plank wall is the lawn
the sun like a prisoner awaiting a death sentence

Colonel Zhang border control   rusted smile
gears grind   for him to climb through a lifetime
and from the corner of his mouth a flash of humanity
I'm the lead in the play   bare bulb   circling
round and round in the whirlpool of night   I sleepwalk—
may the hour of existence spit out silk
a self-spun cocoon more reliable than the universe
my name leads to another name
stage revolves   I chase after me

soliloquy: a jailbreak in Chinese characters
figures cast onto the heavenly canopy   layer after

我正在默讀心跳
在敵意的語義邊界上
鄉音追趕異鄉人
趴在桌上　　渦輪發動機
帶着我半睡半醒的飛行
蟑螂　　地下情報員
沿牆角傳遞上級的信息

黎明轟鳴　　從跑道起飛
按武警戰士的早餐標準 ——
白粥饅頭鹹菜煮雞蛋
兩個隱身人　　輪流照顧我
其中有個詩歌愛好者
詩句與宦途　　指向同一終點
北京時間上午九點五分
國王與馬正式宣讀 ——
我被中國立即驅除出境

一輛大轎車駛進停機坪
武警戰士們下車　　為我開道
穿黑皮夾克　　為失敗而戰
張上校陪同　　前往飛機艙門
從候機廳的機位俯拍
明天一片空白　　影子正撤退
地平線為冬天序曲排練
坐好艙位　　張上校緊緊握手
流動的水銀在艙窗跳躍

layer   I am silently reading my heartbeat
at the boundary of semantic hostility
local accent pursues an outsider
prostrate on the table   turbine engine
bearing my half-asleep half-awake flight
cockroaches   underground intelligence agents
follow the corners of the wall
to pass on information from their superiors

dawn roar   take off from the runway
in accord with the standard breakfast of the armed police—
congee steamed buns pickled vegetables boiled eggs
two invisible men   take turns watching me
one is a lover of poetry
a line of verse and the path of an official   leading
to the same destination
9:05 in the morning Beijing time
the king and the horse formally declaim—
I will be immediately deported from China

a large bus speeds onto the tarmac
armed police step out of the vehicle   clear the way for me
in a black leather jacket   to fight for the defeated
accompanied by Colonel Zhang   toward the airplane door
photographed from a high angle in the waiting area
tomorrow a blank space   shadow retreats
horizon rehearses the winter overture
take a seat in the cabin   Colonel Zhang
gives me a firm handshake
liquid mercury streams down the porthole window

第二十四章

坦克與荊棘　　圍城拉姆安拉
夜的履帶輾壓火的中心
打開古老的地圖　　約旦河以西
一縷春風吹開死者的花朵
穿行橄欖樹　　翻越牆
掠過那隻公雞豎立的羽毛
追趕小毛驢　　辨認雷區
在石井的水槽暢飲

打開新世紀第二頁
耶路撒冷　　諸神在廟山
落腳　　喘口氣　　起飛
衣袖空空　　朝聖者記住信條
以神或人民的名義
鐘擺　　來自內置的原動力
為見證苦難　　蒙上眼
數數瓦罐中的流星

而坦克一寸寸推進
市中心的劇場　　暴風眼
一束追光迎向達爾維什
詞語被照亮　　在水上刻痕
監視器　　不斷放大細節
一秒秒跳動 —— 心臟的位置
坦克逼近母語的防線

阿拉法特　　永遠戴方格頭巾
從鬥士到總統 —— 笑的面具
背向懸崖　　倦於內心刺客
水蓮在總統辦公室沉睡
革命終於追上它的陰影
三天後坦克攻打官邸

XXIV.

tanks and thorns   Ramallah besieged city
treaded tracks of night roll over the heart of fire
spread out the ancient map   west of the Jordan River
a wisp of spring wind opens the flowers of the dead
pass through a grove of olive trees   climb over a wall
hurry by that rooster with raised feathers
chase after a small donkey   mind the minefield
drink freely from the basin of a stone well

open the second page of the new century
Jerusalem   the gods on the Temple Mount
stay for a stretch   gasp for breath   fly away
empty sleeves   pilgrims memorize the creeds
in the name of God or the people
pendulum   arises out of an inner motive force
to witness suffering   cover your eyes
count the meteors in earthen jars

and the tanks advance inch by inch
Al-Kasaba Theatre at the heart of the city   eye of the storm
a spotlight beams down on Darwish
words are illuminated   etched on the water
security cameras   the ceaseless zooming in on details
each second to second pulses—where the heart resides
tanks close in on the line of defense of the mother tongue

Arafat   forever wearing his checkered keffiyeh
from freedom fighter to president—a smiling mask
back against the precipice   weary of the assassin within
water lotus fast asleep at the president's office
revolution eventually catches up with its shadow
three days later tanks attack the official residence

達爾維什對我說 關於自由
詩人與政客的步伐不同

薩拉馬戈一語驚人
盲目　摸索暴君的日子
收割沒有播種的光芒
火山在隱喻中釋放
星星合唱團　推着病床
小溪在課本上一閃而過
屋頂在塵世中漂流
風箏　牽着看不見的手

加沙走廊　炊煙比餓更絕望
沿土路拐彎　歲月悸動
地中海噴吐千萬匹馬的氣息
火柴擦過一生　天空
墜下來 苦難插滿碎玻璃
和記憶綁在一起　硝煙兄弟
逆流追上同源的種族
為諸神乾這杯苦酒

噢達爾維什　你引導我
敲開午夜之門　我的領路人
白色絲巾　呼吸中的母語
而書頁閃動着光芒
從誕生到囚禁　詩歌在生長
為情人品嘗時間之鹽
當暴風雨試圖吹過針眼
他用心臟握緊拳頭

Darwish says to me   *on the matter of freedom*
the pace of poets and politicians are not the same

Saramago astounds with a word
Blindness   groping fumbling despot days
harvests the light it didn't sow
volcano in metaphor set free
sidereal chorus   pushes the hospital bed
rivulets shimmer across the textbook
rooftops drift along the world of dust
a kite   pulls the unseen hands

Gaza corridor   cooking smoke more desperate than hunger
follow the dirt road around a corner   years throb
the Mediterranean Sea exhales the breath of ten million horses
a match strikes for a lifetime   sky
crashes down   suffering fills with shards of glass
becomes bound to memory   brothers in gunsmoke
fighting the current to chase the homogenous race
dry this bitter cup of wine for the gods

O Darwish   you guide me along the track
knocking on the gate of midnight   my torchbearer
white scarf   mother tongue centers the breath
and the pages of the book flicker with light
from birth to imprisonment   poetry grows
for lovers to savor the salt of time
when the hurricane tries to blow through the eye of a needle
he uses the heart to make a fist

第二十五章

阿連德總統在獨立廳
用自動步槍對準自己下頜
結束生命 —— 大海翻轉過來
天空傾斜　星雲湧動

北京燕山某建築工地
我攥住小報　為智利而哭
正午時分　草帽與太陽相稱
鐵鍬　帶汗鹹的工作服
中國苦力　深挖時間的陰影
弓起脊背馱運群山
全世界無產者聯合起來 ——
二十四歲呵我的熱血

向南半球逆行奔走呼喊
午夜吞噬太陽 屍體
推向初生的波浪　地平線 ——
柔情之刃　為了守望一生

一九七三年九月十一日上午
聶魯達病重　正聽新聞廣播
—— 這是法西斯主義
墨西哥總統派專機接聶魯達
他要死在自己的土地上

十月的天空　我來到智利
幽靈在石碑重逢　點亮熄滅的燈
子彈與歲月　二十五萬人流亡
遠行的鑰匙找不到回家的鎖
詞的蜂群　被過度闡釋的人蜇傷
當初少年是一張白紙
鉛筆雨線　新月的犁直到邊界

XXV.

President Allende in Independence Hall
points an automatic rifle under his chin
and ends his life—the ocean flips over
the sky tilts down   clouds of stars surge

construction site in the Yan Mountains Beijing
I grasp the current *Reference News*   and weep for Chile
noon hour   straw hat to match the sun
shovel   work clothes soaked with sweat
Chinese *coolie*   digs deep into the shadow of time
carrying the mountains on your bent back
workers of the world unite—
O my boiling blood age twenty-four

run shouting against the tide toward the Southern Hemisphere
midnight swallows the sun   dead bodies
push against the nascent wave   horizon line—
knife blade of tenderness   to keep watch over a lifetime
the morning of September 11, 1973
Neruda severely ill   listens to a news broadcast
—"this is fascism"
the president of Mexico sends a plane to pick him up
Neruda wants to die in his own homeland

October sky   I've arrived in Chile
ghosts reunite at the stone stele   light the extinguished lamp
bullets and the years   25,000 people forced into exile
the far-flung key can't find the lock to return home
a swarm of words   stung by the overinterpreters
early youth is a blank sheet of paper
pencil rain lines   the plow of the crescent moon reaches the border

戒嚴　　急救車呼嘯而過
在聖地亞哥的街道
士兵們持槍兩次攔截搜查
聶魯達　　滿臉流淚
太平洋拍擊着船長†的棺材

建築工地的大工棚
通鋪第二層　　遮暗的燈光下
我讀聶魯達的詩　　寫筆記
兇手早已消失　　鐘聲

滾動的是天空還是大海
愛情與革命　　正如火的描述
熱烈耀眼而轉瞬即逝
愛情 —— 最多會組成家庭
革命 —— 和大眾和權力有關
往往變成暴力與專制

一九七二年二月　　尼克松
和周恩來在北京機場握手
用報紙捲煙　　跟師傅借火
無端的疾風從哪兒來
大街上女人的領口露出顏色
袖口綠了　　柳樹舒展懶腰

苦難碾壓過來　　淹沒尖叫
綠色美元在印鈔機運轉
尼克松和基辛格從幕後轉身
我們的手沒有露出來

森林的箭簇射向黎明
發條擰緊的心臟驟然停止
祖國　　死者想抽支煙
從天空剪出小鳥　　召喚我

martial law   emergency vehicles wail by
on a street in Santiago
stopped and searched twice by soldiers with guns
Neruda   face full of tears
the Pacific Ocean pounds on the captain's coffin

at a construction site in a provisional workers' tent
second-floor bunks   under a dim light
I read Neruda's poetry   take notes
murderers vanished long ago   bell tolls

is that rumbling the sky or the sea
love and revolution   like a description of fire
ardor blazes and fades in a fleeting instant
love—at most can make a family
revolution—relates to the masses and power
often turns violent and authoritarian

February 1972   Nixon
and Zhou Enlai shake hands at the Beijing airport
newsprint used to roll a cigarette
lighter borrowed from the foreman
from where does this wild blast of wind blow
the necklines of women bare colors on the avenue
sleeve cuffs green   willow trees stretch and unfurl

suffering steamrolls on   drowns the screams
green dollars roll round and round the printing machines
Nixon and Kissinger turn around behind the scenes—
our hand doesn't show on this one though

arrows shoot out from the forest toward dawn
windup spring heart suddenly stops
ancestorland   the dead want to smoke a cigarette
little birds cut out of the sky   beckoning me

最後一夜　　和詩人們相聚
紅酒照亮命運的時刻
四位智利詩人　　三個坐過牢
含着淚的何塞對我說
你面前是牆　　但必須穿過去
那是我們世界的倒影

my last night   gathering with the poets
red wine brightens the moment of fate
four Chilean poets   three were imprisoned
with tears in his eyes José says to me
   —there's a wall in front of you   but you must pass
through   that image is a reflection of our world

第二十六章

停屍房　　勞富林辨認迪蘭的屍體
半文盲的姑娘確定身份 —— 寫過詩
瘋狂的迪蘭　　鴿群帶動教堂旋轉

在海邊聽見黑色元音的鳥群

金沙在沙漏中 —— 時代的恐懼
無窮動的股票波浪　　追上沉船殘月
塗鴉和岩畫沒人簽名　　繼續攀登
從藝術家生涯到自由落體
曼哈頓管樂隊為哈德遜河送葬

我打開雨傘　　為了生存倒退

有人宿醉　　用恨吹開牽牛花
默片慢動作　　逆歷史方向而行
在死亡線擱淺　　書籍聳立
穿過語言的隧道　　沒有出口

艾略特　　我的同齡兄弟
不同的搖籃　　陌生的海洋
我們在龜島不期而遇
他書中的狂風　　讓我四處漂泊
影子傾斜　　追趕神話的正午

趕上永別前最後的一站

正午搭乘長島火車
翻開《紐約時報》　　上下顛倒
被另一種語言遮蔽世界
我夢見北京動物園的獅子
頭一堂課　　英文是劊子手的斧頭
冷颼颼　　中文腦袋居然還在

XXVI.

at the morgue   Laughlin identifies Dylan Thomas's corpse
a semiliterate young girl confirms it—"he wrote poems"
mad Dylan   a flock of pigeons sets the church spinning

by the sea's side hear the dark-vowelled birds

gold sand fills the hourglass—a time of terror
constantly shifting waves of stocks and shares   catch up
with the shipwrecked sliver of moon   no one signs
graffiti or petroglyphs   keep climbing   from the artist's life
to freefall   Manhattan honking band funeral march for the Hudson Rive

I open an umbrella   to survive the backward descent

someone with a hangover   blows open a morning glory
silent film in slow-motion   walking in the opposite direction of history
runs aground on the precipice of death   books rise into towers
crossing through the tunnel of language   there's no exit

Eliot   my birthyear brother
different cradles   unfamiliar ocean
we meet by chance on Turtle Island
the wild winds in his books   let me drift and moor in the four directions
shadows slant   chasing after the noonday of myths

catch the last stop before the final parting

riding the noon train out to Long Island
open the *New York Times*   upside down
the world obscured by another type of language
I dream about the lions at the Beijing Zoo
the first day of class   English the executioner's ax
so bitingly cold   Chinese somehow still in the brain

在石溪與楊振寧相遇

一對一輔導課　　盲人領着明眼人
詩歌製造　　在流水線盡頭 ——
臥室的鏡子　　打開語言保險櫃
遛狗　　可別忘了帶上自己

日子紛飛　　中國作家討論會
艾略特主持　　帕斯†夫婦在聽眾中
我們和帕斯夫婦一起吃晚飯
燭火　　三種語言的走馬燈
天安門　　冷戰　　美洲政治與文學
關於聶魯達　　帕斯搖搖頭
僭越了政治與道德的準則

我追趕一個人，他跌倒
又爬起來，看見我說，沒人。

中國獨立電影節開幕式
薩格斯管潛入夜　　吐露溪流
用詞垂釣　　引來想像外的彗星
觀眾進入比光更大的空間
大雪落下　　虛無的重量
在林肯中心的池塘打水漂
而尊嚴比失敗的事業更偉大

拳頭突然釋放隱喻
兩個赤裸的姑娘穿過銀幕
向鄰居的演員借衣服 潛入地下
時代與暗流 —— 氣象員永遠年輕
他們是風 描述風的形狀

你用不着氣象員告知風往哪兒吹

at Stony Brook meet C. N. Yang

one-on-one tutorials   the blind man leading the bright-eyed
poetry manufacturing   at the end of the assembly line—
bedroom mirror   crack open the language vault
walk the dog   but don't forget to bring yourself along

days flap away   symposium for Chinese writers in exile
Eliot moderates   Octavio and Marie-José Paz in the audience
we eat dinner together   candle flames   three-language carousel
Tiananmen   Cold War   American politics and literature
concerning Neruda's odes to Stalin   Paz shakes his head—
"transgressed political and ethical principles"

I pursue someone, he tumbles, gets back
up again, sees me and says, No one

China Independent Film Festival opening ceremony
saxophone dives into the night   uncovers a stream
using words to fish   reel in the comet beyond imagination
the audience enters a space larger than light
heavy snowfall   weight of nothingness
skip stones on the reflecting pool at Lincoln Center
and dignity more important than a failed cause

a clenched fist suddenly sets metaphor free

after the explosion   two women survivors stagger
out of the movie screen   naked toward an actress neighbor
they borrow clothes   go into hiding
the times and the undercurrent—Weathermen forever young
they are the wind   describe the shape of the wind

you don't need a weatherman to know which way the wind blows

旗幟的顏色變幻　　向暮色致敬
夜騎燈光過河　　警車拐角呼嘯而過
杯子碎了　　水的形狀依然存在

逃亡　　我繞過每一個祖國

邁克像鳥閉上眼　　為了讓天空消失
擁抱雨擁抱切分音的時光
而他母親的大鐘被繼父賣掉
紐約人　　紐約卻一無所有

寫作是為了抹去一行行的詩句

flags change colors   salute the twilight   night
rides the lamplight across the river   police cars wail around
a corner   a glass shatters   the shape of the water remains

in exile   I detour away from every homeland

M. March shuts his eyes like a bird   to make the sky disappear
embraces the rain embraces the syncopation of time
as his stepfather sells his mother's grandfather clock
a New Yorker   in New York left with nothing

writing as a way to erase line after line of poetry

第二十七章

楚瓦什男孩拎着煤油燈
黑夜鏟除白雪 —— 莫斯科
明信片：背後是風暴
與帕斯捷尔納克為鄰
艾基被高尔基文學院開除
沒有身份證　　影子代表自己
在火車站過夜　　扳道工
火車頭偏離的方向 ——

鹿特丹的天空讓我分神
黃銅舵輪與旋轉木馬
艾基成了悲喜劇的主角
宋琳在紙上複製一條小河
記憶的錨露出中文水面
抽煙的張棗手舞足蹈
每個穿盔甲的詞
正如棋路　在暴君的手中

夏天抓住它尾巴　　哥本哈根
樹影　　光的葉子飄飛
我們倆在作家學校講課
法官博魯姆穿針引線
只有一種舊感覺的
白銀 —— 當自由的溫暖與肩上
我和艾基夫婦乾杯
沉默放大星空的音量

柏林之春　　顧城夫婦家
戴高筒帽做飯　　他談論死亡
魚的快樂　　盤子　　盤子
為我領路　　從三層到底樓
敲開艾基夫婦的門

XXVII.

a Chuvash boy carries a kerosene lamp
shovels snow through the night—Moscow
postcard: storm in the background
and Pasternak as neighbor   Gennady
Aygi expelled from the Gorky Literary Institute
no identification card   shadow represents itself
spends the night at the train station   switchman
the diverted track of the locomotive

Rotterdam sky divides my attention
brass ship's wheel and carousel
Aygi becomes the lead in a tragicomic translation play
Song Lin reproduces a small river on paper
the anchor of memory reveals the water surface of Chinese
Zhang Zao smokes as his hands dance feet stamp
each word puts on its armor
like a chess move   in the hands of a tyrant

summer grabs its tail   Copenhagen
tree shadows   leaves of light flit through the air
the two of us teaching at the Writers' School
Judge Borum our intercessor threads the needle
only a kind of silver
of ancient feeling—in the warmth of freedom on the shoulders
I dry cups with Gennady and his wife Galina
silence amplifies the sound waves of the starry sky

Berlin spring   at Gu Cheng and Xie Ye's apartment
the poet cooks in his tall pant-leg hat   talks about death
happiness of fish   dish   to dish
leads the way for me   from the third to the ground floor
knock on the Aygis' door

詞與詞坐在一起 顧城是
空格　　用冬天的手勢
貼近靈魂的雪花

教堂林立　　鐘聲激烈爭論
柏洛伊特詩歌節　　頭髮
如灰燼的火焰　　他用熊抱
緊摟住白樺樹和我
我們正追趕世界的盡頭
在歲月變成石雕以前
閉幕式　　他在朗讀《雪》
椅子，雪，睫毛，燈。

他參加我的詩歌創作課
窗與世界　　轉向上游
追上楚瓦什語的發音
風吹着生者與死者的排簫
在俄語的詩歌韻律中
調音師　　夢也是危險的
而漢字集權於天下
舞龍　　鱗片閃閃發光

他給生死線的朋友寫信
穿過遺忘穿過田野
旋風成歌　　寂寞的火花
為了展示地平線的時間
太陽熨平母親河的
褶皺　　樹根暢飲光芒
那等待砍伐的森林
有斧子的憂鬱

word sits together with word   Gu Cheng is
a blank space   using the gestures of winter
to nestle close to the snowflowers of the soul

forest of churches   bells peal fierce arguments
at the Beloit Poetry Festival   hair
like flames of ash   Gennady gives a bear hug
embracing the white birches and me
we chase after the ends of the world
before the years become carved stone
at the closing ceremony   he reads "Snow"
chair , snow , eyelashes , lamp

he comes to my poetry workshop
window and world   swerve upstream
in pursuit of Chuvash intonation
wind blows the panpipes of the living and the dead
in the prosody of Russian verse
tuner   dreams are also dangerous
while Chinese characters centralize power under heaven
dragon dance   scales shimmer and shine

he writes a letter to a friend at death's door
crosses oblivion   crosses the fields
whirlwind becomes song   lonely spark
to reveal the hour of the horizon line
the sun irons out the wrinkles
of the Mother River   tree roots drink up the blades of light
that forest waiting to be cut down
feels the melancholy of the ax

第二十八章

童謠的北京　　我回來了
城門城門幾丈高
光與魔術是城的變奏
死亡裁縫用夜剪裁山河
誰高舉我名字的牌子 ──
首都機場　　便衣們向我致敬

據點　鷹在鳥巢孵恐龍蛋
客廳的針孔鏡頭對準我
集中思想　　隔壁是音樂學院
音階繼續攀升　　亮出
管弦樂隊的大鑔　　向日葵
帝國中軸線　黃曆　　鳥
看見我行走的童年

踮着雙腳移動　　嚴文井
打開威士忌　燈光紡着暮色
我緊緊摟住樹神的牛漢
觸摸蔡其矯手中的火花
病房解凍　　馮亦代‡露出光腳
在歧路的盡頭喚醒我

在最後的門檻轉身 ──
謊言與真實編織的河流
字眼的鉚釘加固船底
房檐翹起　　停泊在天涯外
咳嗽追逐烏鴉　　而風鈴乍起
傾聽父親 ── 背影

公雞不再相信黎明 ──
餐廳　無電梯無殘疾通道
輪椅上的魏斐德被抬起來

XXVIII.

Beijing of nursery rhymes   I've returned
city gate city gate how high how tall
light and magic are the musical variations of the city
the Tailor of Death uses the night to alter the mountains and rivers
someone lifts a sign with my name overhead—
Capitol Airport   plainclothesmen salute me

secret base   the eagle on the Bird's Nest hatches a dinosaur egg
pinhole camera in the living room stares at me
gathering thoughts   music conservatory next door
scales keep climbing   unleash luminous
orchestral cymbals   sunflowers
imperial central axis   divination calendar   birds
watch my childhood walk away

move along on tiptoe   Yan Wenjing
opens a bottle of whisky   lamplight spins threads of twilight
I tightly embrace the tree deity Niu Han
touch the sparks in Cai Qijiao's hands
hospital ward thaws   Feng Yidai barefoot
wakes me up at the end of the sidetrack

turn around at the last threshold—
river woven with lies and truth
word-rivets brace the boat's hull
eaves curve up   anchor drops beyond the end of sky
coughs pursue crows   and the windbells rise *qingting qingting*
listening closely to Father—from behind his shadow

the rooster no longer believes in dawn—
restaurant   no elevator no passageway for the disabled
Fred Wakeman in a wheelchair lifted inside

一個個菜從風景撤走
歷史在告別的橋下分流

醒來　　影子追趕我
我追趕早已發出的書信
書信追趕意外的白馬
白馬追趕繩索中的厄運
厄運追趕所有鐘錶
鐘錶追趕回歸的路程

午夜　　黃銳在門外送客
我正對準北斗七星
想想有多少朝代興衰
老頭練太極拳　　準備升天
鄉愁　　步話機頻道

月亮護士照顧所有病人
沿着改道的護城河
後海品嘗味精的孤獨
吊車正組裝夜的部件
群鴉變成黑色的雪
我被匿名　　獵人也沒有名字

忠實於冬天的情人
更換二十四節氣的衣裳
時間在玻璃杯口傾斜
我從秘密約會的拐角歸來
從門走廊直到陽台 ——

童謠的北京　　我回來了
十三年 —— 世紀裂縫
而母語讓我更陌生
兔子的季節　　追趕綠皮火車
午夜溢出黎明的河
大地的婚床　　喇叭嗚咽

dish after dish retreats from the landscape
the flow of history diverts under the bridge of parting

waking up   a shadow chases me
chases the open letter issued long ago
the letter chases the white horse of chance
the white horse chases misfortune in the reins
misfortune chases all the clocks
the clocks chase the way back

midnight   Huang Rui sees the guest out the door
I align myself with the Seven Stars of the Northern Dipper
thinking about how many dynasties have risen and fallen
the old man practices tai chi   preparing to ascend to heaven
homesickness   frequency on a walkie-talkie

the moon nurses take care of all the sick patients
along the rechanneled city moat
Houhai Lake tastes the loneliness of MSG
cranes assemble the components of the night
a flock of crows turns into black snow
my name erased   the hunter too is nameless

faithful to the winter lover
change the clothes of the twenty-four solar terms
time tilts at the mouth of the glass
I return from the corner of the secret date
from the gate passageway reach the terrace—

Beijing of nursery rhymes   I've returned
thirteen years—the century cracks
and the mother tongue has deepened my foreignness
season of the rabbit   chases the green-skinned train
midnight spills over the river of dawn
wedding bed of the world   horns weeping

第二十九章

靈魂出竅 —— 車禍
八十號公路爬上二〇〇五年夏天
從戴維斯到薩克拉門托
流星剎車　　請回放 ——
失重　　夜的洗衣機在旋轉
小號吐出一串串泡沫

天邊　　救護車呼嘯而來
找到眼鏡 —— 顛倒的地平線
樂隊指揮篡改總譜
我向遠方的親人招手 ——

沿着時間軸打開私人空間
二〇〇二年晚秋在五十號公路染色
從柏洛伊特到戴維斯
肩上群山移動　　展現夜的
秩序　　星群在思路偏離

加油站 —— 罐裝風暴
進入沙漠　　我乞求愛的荒涼
地圖捲起扎了根的小鎮
從後視鏡回望落日
腹地　　火光追逐印第安人
風在雕塑地貌與人類

黑戰士河進入青銅的黎明
二十號公路迎向二〇〇五年新春
林中老宅　　教授夫婦的骨灰
放在前花園的石壇下
數數四個房間　　從不同窗戶
月亮對準失眠的客人

XXIX.

soul escapes through orifice—car crash
Interstate 80 climbs the summer of 2005
driving from UC Davis to Sacramento
a meteor brakes   please replay—
weightlessness   night's washing machine spins
trumpet spits out bubble after bubble

edge of sky   ambulance sirens close in
eyeglasses found—horizon upside down
orchestra conductor tampering with the score
I wave to distant family

follow the time line to open private spaces
2002 late autumn dyes its colors onto Route 50
driving from Beloit to Davis   mountains
move atop my shoulders   unfolding night's
order   asterisms wander off from lines of thought

gas station—canned storm
entering the desert   I beg for love's desolation
the map rolls up the little town that took root
gazing at the setting sun in the rearview mirror
hinterland   firelight chases the American Indians
wind sculpts the topography as well as humanity

Black Warrior River flows into the bronze dawn
Interstate 20 welcomes me into the spring of 2005
old house in the Alabama woods   ashes of the married professors
placed before a stone altar in the front garden
count the four rooms   through different windows
the moon aims at the insomniac guest

沒被王者的石頭擊中
南方口音糾正我的英文
我帶上雨傘散步　　烈犬咆哮
欄杆守衛南方的太陽
狩獵詩歌課　　我蹲在英文牢籠
為保持安全的距離
艾略特發現第五個房間 ——

語言的內部　　我閉上眼
閃電擊中樹根　　水滴穿石
韻律是有形的慾望
你叫喊　　時代沒有回聲

九十四號公路抵達二○○六年寒冬
從芝加哥機場到南灣
哥特式建築群在白紙上
站立　　我排隊等教授的位置
穿越體制半透明的牆

我的靈魂倒退一九九四年夏天
正在學開車　　集中精力
從安娜堡到底特律機場
準備飛翔　　夢中的跑道
加速　　海鷗迎來　　密西根湖
在絕望的漏斗傾斜

來自世界末日的推銷員
敲門　　我在失業中寫作
推動那些貓的日子
烏鴉在市中心的樹上開會

夏天行進在八十號公路
從一一三號公路轉拉索大道
華燈濕潤　　這是我的家 ——
歷史以外的避難所
陪我的女兒長大成人

the king's stone didn't hit me
Southern accent corrects my English
I take an umbrella on a walk   a mean dog snarls and growls
the railing guards the Southern sun
hunting poetry class   I crouch in the cage of English
in order to preserve a safe distance
Eliot discovers the fifth room—

the inside of language   I close my eyes
lightning strikes tree roots   waterdrops pierce into rock
rhythm is a tangible desire
you cry out   the epoch has no echo

Interstate 94 reaches the winter of 2006
from Chicago O'Hare to South Bend
Gothic architecture crowds onto a blank page
standing   I line up and wait for the professor's chair
pass through the system's translucent walls

my soul travels back to the summer of 1994
learning to drive   focused energy
from Ann Arbor to Detroit Airport
getting ready to fly   runway in a dream
accelerate   seagulls welcome   Lake Michigan
banking in the funnel of desperation

salesman arrives from the end of the world
knocks on the door   I write while unemployed
push those cat days forward
crows hold a meeting in a tree at the center of the city

summer advances to Interstate 80
from Highway 113 turn onto Russell Boulevard
the lanterns are damp   this is my home—
refuge outside of history where
I am with my daughter growing up

第三十章

冬夜　　內華達山脈　　深林
蓋瑞提馬燈　　取木柴
火是心跳　　他坐進空谷中
土狼們追着長長的信

反精神污染運動追着我
一九八四年晚秋　　他與艾倫
和我在竹園賓館秘密見面
哨音鑽透夢的天藍
房瓦鋪蓋着虛構的夜

伐木工　　水手　　守林員
你是靜坐中盤旋的思想
棲居在京都相國寺 ——
風鈴與蟋蟀互相應和

他請我上一堂詩歌課
野外　　學生玩語言遊戲
帕幽塔的陽光讓我分心
印第安人逐水而居
帶鱗的日子穿網而過

夥計　　為你打抱不平
有人把我排擠到系統以外
我和印第安人都沒有家
流浪　　在美國流浪

小母牛死了　　男孩很傷心
走到教堂　　牧師搖搖頭 ——
小母牛不能上天堂
他再也不信基督教了
佛教即眾生平等

XXX.

winter night   Sierra Nevada Mountains   deep forest
Gary raises the kerosene lamp   fetches firewood
fire is the heartbeat   he sits in the empty valley
coyotes chase a long letter

anti-spiritual pollution campaign chases me
late fall 1984   he and Allen
meet me in secret at the Bamboo Garden Hotel
whistles drill through the sky blue of dream
roof tiles blanket the fictitious night

woodcutter   seaman   forester
you are the mind circling in meditation
dwelling in Kyoto's Shokokuji Temple—
wind chimes and crickets echo each other

he invited me to join a poetry class
wilderness   students playing language games
sunlight on Putah Creek distracting me
American Indians who lived here near the waters
fish-scale days passed through the net

"comrades fight for you when you've been wronged"
some people threw me out of the system
both the American Indians and I have lost a home
drifting   drifting   in America

the young heifer died   the little boy so heartbroken
walks to church   the priest shakes his head—
No the young heifer cannot enter Heaven
the boy has lost his faith in Christianity
Buddhism assumes the equality of all living things

內華達城外　　我們迷了路
尋找顛倒地圖的星星
他領路　　穿過房間與森林
細雨　　織着早春的布

日式禪堂　　靈魂的住所
他在香案盤坐　　焚香合十
擊磬　　搖鈴　　敲龜殼
色即是空　　空即是色
收盡土地山谷森林和鳥

斧柄是動詞的延伸
年輪自述可疑的歲月
他劈開木柴　　過冬
千隻紙鶴越過愛的群山

越過太平洋　　我領路
從香港島到詩歌節碼頭
他在甲板打坐　　我睡着了
大海直立　　眾生浮雕——
人類病態的幻象

媽祖廟　　香火繚繞
他用簡單手勢代替語言
推開一扇扇悲喜之門
無性　　在呼與吸之間

三人行　　虛線也是歸途
在白鴿巢公園山坡上
圍坐石桌旁而論天下
夜暮垂落　　棋盤反轉
禪與山河對弈——

somewhere outside Nevada City   we lose our way
search the stars in the upside-down map
he leads the way   passing through room and forest
misty rain   weaves the cloth of early spring

zazen room   abode of the soul   he sits cross-legged
before the meditation table   lights incense presses palms to the heart
strikes the chimes   shakes the bell   raps the tortoise shell
form is emptiness   emptiness is form
receives the wholeness of the land valley forest and birds

an axe handle is an extension of a verb
growth rings recount their own suspicious years
he splits firewood   to get through winter
a thousand paper cranes cross mountains of love

crossing the Pacific Ocean   I lead the way
from Hong Kong Island to the poetry festival port
he meditates on deck   I fall asleep
ocean rises vertically   all living beings sculpted in relief—
the sickness of humanity an illusion

Mazu Temple   incense smoke curls into the air
he uses simple hand gestures in place of spoken words
pushing open door after door of sorrow and happiness
No Nature   between exhalation and inhalation

three of us cross the border   a broken line is also the way back home
on the hillside at White Dove Nest Park
we sit around a stone table and talk about the world
night falls   the chessboard flips over
dhyana plays a game with the mountains and rivers—

我掀開那夜幕一角
他喊一聲，起身，站定
而向激流和山巒
舉起雙手，高呼三次！

I lift up a corner from that curtain of night:
He cries out, rises up and stands
Facing toward the torrent and the mountain
Raises up both hands and shouts three times!

第三十一章

太陽在躍動　　白洋淀 ——
風吹蘆葦　　船搖過天空
一九八二年初夏　　安達壯一
宿醉　　我們沒有槳
新婚後　　他和炊煙一起
從北京胡同伸懶腰

東京　　《今天》二十週年
從結局到出發的路上
語言的暴君抓狂
日本詩人們為漢詩遠行
讓觀眾像潮水般退去
裸露的是錨的記憶

金閣寺在黃皮書閃現
那僧徒放了一把火 ——
三島由紀夫領悟瞬間的美
用刀鋒劈開水的憂愁
櫻花散落在托盤上

彈球機讓我熱血沸騰
閃光雷鳴　　向命運學徒
我組裝的零件被控制
而鋼珠滾進漏斗中

中日連詩 —— 千年之海
首尾銜接　　排浪與排浪
我遠望富士山發呆
心臟病與廣島原子彈
中年危機　　我無處可逃
向八面風鞠躬 ——

XXXI.

the sun pulses   Baiyang Lake—
wind blows the reeds   boat rocks across the sky
early summer 1982   Adachi Souichi
hungover   we have no oars
just married   he stretches out with the cooking smoke
in a hutong alley in Beijing

Tokyo   twentieth anniversary of *Today* magazine
on the road from the end to the start of the journey
the tyrants of language go crazy
how far Japanese poets travel for Chinese poetry
the audience recedes like tidewater
exposing the anchor's memories

Kinkakuji Temple flickers in the pages of the yellow cover book
set ablaze by the young Buddhist monk—
Mishima Yukio   grasps ephemeral beauty
splits the sorrows of water with a blade
sakura petals scatter on a tray

pachinko machine makes my blood surge
a flash and thunder   apprentice to fate
all the parts I've assembled have been taken over
as the steel balls roll into the chute

China-Japan unite poetries—"seas of the millennium"
end to end connect   wave into wave
I gaze dazed at Mount Fuji in the distance
heart disease and the Hiroshima bomb
midlife crisis   nowhere for me to flee
bow before the eight directions of the wind—

歲月洗白是永駿的頭髮
我日本的影子在遊蕩
福田的車轍被喚醒 ──
童年　　瘦小的身影在飲水
中學讀魯迅的《野草》
翻過語言柵欄的危險

京都之靜　　寺廟之小
星星的骰子在夜空滾動
野鹿追隨我的女兒
光的經文　　聾的花朵
那前世的太陽在溫泉中

我的影子繼續流浪
伊豆沒有舞女雨更大
撐開音律的油布傘
隧道盡頭　　光蝴蝶迎來

東京大轟炸廢墟
一棵小樹在妄想中生長
扎根　　一代代的警報
正沿着地鐵滾梯向上
迎向星球博物館

為什麼建自己的詩碑
淋透的心情　　我穿雨靴
泥濘小路直到世界盡頭
缺席比爭辯更持久──
詩的靈魂暫住石頭中

我去看望谷川俊太郎
在他出生的老宅
鉛筆的桅桿　　白紙的風暴
二十億光年的孤獨
茶杯　水　渦流　火星文

Shun Korenaga's hair washed white by the years
my Japanese shadow wanders around
car tracks awakened in Fukude fields—
childhood   a slight figure drinks water
reads Lu Xun's *Wild Grass* in middle school
the dangers of climbing over the stockades of language

Kyoto stillness   little temple
the dice of the stars roll in the night sky
a wild deer follows my daughter
sutra of light   deaf flowers
sun from a past life in the hot spring

my shadow continues to roam
Izu has no *dancing girl*   rain falls harder
opens the rhythm's oilcloth umbrella
end of a tunnel   greeting butterflies of light

ruins from the firebombing of Tokyo
a small tree grows in the middle of delusion
taking root   alarm signals through the generations
on the subway escalator going up   to the planetarium

why erect your own poetry monument
at Kamogawa City   rain-soaked mood
I wear rubber boots   muddy trail reaches the end of the world
absence lasts longer than debate—
the spirit of poetry lives transiently in stone

I pay a visit to Tanikawa Shuntaro
at the old house in which he was born
pencil mast   blank paper storm
two billion light years of loneliness
teacup   water   whirlpool   Mars-speak

第三十二章

兩個東方文明的對話 ——
喜馬拉雅　　冰海堆積成高峰
亞洲農耕文明的版圖
新德里　　印度國際中心
中印作家就長桌而坐

艾倫陪我們穿過寡婦村
太陽停擺　　苦難的刻度
沙麗纏裹女性的一生
花的肌理　　從綻放到凋謝
猴子從艾倫背後偷走
眼鏡　　在廟頂靜觀 ——

沒有玻璃的小旅館
展開午夜的透明的肺
蚊子和我們一起去旅行
婚禮的歌聲從遠到近
露出黎明的馬腳

瓦拉納西　　恒河的落日
火把成龍　　波浪的動與靜
寺廟正向我們漂移
赤腳戴花環　　我和馬格利斯
有人帶路　　他向眾神捐款
抹掉滿臉汗水　　轉向我

恒河　　閃電與土地的氣息
祈禱　　洗澡　　舞蹈　　火葬
內心的油燈照亮我的皮膚
難道眾神先於種姓制度
閃光的種子撒向夜空

XXXII.

"a conversation between two Eastern civilizations"—
Himalayas   seas of ice heap into peaks
the zone of farming civilization in Asia
New Delhi   India International Centre
Chinese & Indian writers sit at a conference table

I. Allan Sealy takes us to Vrindavan the city of widows
sun halts   the scale of suffering
a sari winds around the lifetime of a woman
the texture of flowers   from blossoming to withering away
a monkey sneaks behind Allan and steals his
eyeglasses   looks calmly out from the temple roof

little hotel without glass
expands the transparent lungs of midnight
mosquitoes go on a trip with us
distant singing from a wedding draws near
betraying the cloven hooves of dawn

Varanasi   sun sets on the Ganges
flames turn into a dragon   the motion and stillness of waves
a temple drifts toward us
Magris and I   barefoot and garlanded with flowers
people lead the way   he leaves a dāna for the gods
wipes the dripping sweat from his face   and turns to me

Ganges   breath of lightning and the land
prayer   bathing   dancing   cremation
the heart's oil lamp illuminates my skin
did the gods precede the caste system
shimmering seeds scatter into the night sky

鹿野苑　　菩提樹在哪兒
我迷戀於死的恐懼
玄奘正穿行移動的邊界
經幡飛揚　　佛經到中國
寺廟們撐住老百姓的風雨
數數日子的念珠——

中印作家對話在繼續
蒼蠅在時間上打滑
午餐　　一隻大烏鴉俯衝
搶走歐陽江河的美食
轉向主題與變奏

埃洛拉石窟第十六窟
多少代人日夜鑿穿巨石
建築師看到紙上風景
我像盲人　　觸摸門廊盡頭
工匠雕刻我的眼睛——

藍色之城　　從城堡俯瞰
深井是國王的孤獨
近水口渴　　金酒杯是
緘默　　我和女兒騎駱駝
沙漠才是時間的廣告
日與影　　怎麼描述風

吉普賽人　　自由的祖先
種姓制度中不可接觸的人
我們品嘗大麻餅乾
追趕帳篷追趕風的家鄉

第四輪中印作家對話
香港　　暴風雨前夜的寧靜
準備好不同的風球
飛鳥轉向桂花香的時刻
西湖　　我們和泰戈爾合影

Deer Park   where is the Bodhi Tree
I am enchanted by the fear of death
Xuanzang passing through shifting borders
prayer flags fly up   Buddhist sutras reach China
the temples sustain the lives of the people through wind and rain
count the mala beads of the days—

the conversation between Chinese & Indian writers continues
flies slipping in time
at lunch   a large crow swoops down
and snatches away Ouyang Jianghe's tasty meal
swerves into our themes and variations

Ellora Kailasa temple Cave 16
how many generations chiseled the basalt day night day
the architect sees the landscape on paper
I'm like a blind man   feeling the edge of the vestibule
the artisans carve my eyes—

Blue City   looking out from the castle fort
a deep well is the solitude of kings
thirsting near water   the golden cups are
silent   I ride a camel with my daughter
the desert is an advertisement for time
sun and shadow   how can you describe the wind

Rajasthani nomads   ancestors of freedom
untouchable ones of the caste system
we taste the bhang cookies
chase the canvas tents chase the homeland of the wind

fourth round of conversations between Chinese & Indian writers
Hong Kong   the peacefulness of the night before a tropical rainstorm
prepare for different typhoon warning signals
birds veer into the hour of osmanthus redolence
West Lake   we take a group photo with Tagore

第三十三章

就像桿秤的棧橋突然傾斜　　遊船四散　　喧囂的
鳥群　　太陽的高音喇叭被放大　　林蔭道跟上死
神的步調　　招來另一個世界的出租車　　緊急出
口的火的標誌　　戴大口罩的白色天使像雲朵飄
動　　沿走廊直到世界秩序的終點　　你叫什麼名
字　　被半透明的章魚綁架——

漫長的一夜　　托起語言石頭的重量　　醒來是
天花板的溜冰場　　　模仿日子的兩個小丑互
相追趕　　鄉音躺在遠方的乾草垛上　　馬群突破
死亡的圍欄　　我用手機給助教發短信——亂
碼　　咿咿呀呀　　我重新開始學中文　　女兒在
教我看圖識字　　穿過不同班級之間通用的病句

語言障礙專家的判斷是對的　　　我真的甘願
送披薩　　緊跟着踏上音階的狂人　　陽光一閃
——我停止寫作　　拉鍊的小路露出夜的脊背
等待記憶主人的鞭打　　鬥雞眼的皇帝在山河長
卷盡頭蓋上玉璽

星雲般墨點在宣紙上——與宇宙相稱　　畫畫
讓我狂喜　　墨點聚散依附錯落流動　　森林在
語言邊界之外　　　禍兮福之所倚福兮禍之所伏
我是沒有靶標的自由　　傾聽雪花的低語　　守望
日與夜渦旋中的神秘河流

XXXIII.

as if the steelyard's landing stage suddenly tilted   pleasure boats
disperse   a ruckus of birds   the loudspeaker of the sun has been
amplified   the shady boulevard keeps up with the god of death
hail a taxi from another world   emergency fire exit sign   white
angels wearing large masks float like clouds   follow the corridor
to the end of the world order   what is your name   abducted by
the translucent devilfish

endless night   lift the weight of the language stone   waking up
to an ice rink on the ceiling   the two clowns who mime the days
chase each other   sounds of home lie flat on the distant haystack
a herd of horses breaks through death's fenceline   I text my teach-
ing assistant—garbled signs   *babble babble   blubble   burble*
I begin to learn Chinese all over again   my daughter teaches me
with learn-to-read flash cards   working through many common
grade school grammatical mistakes

the speech-language pathologist's assessment is correct   I'm
really ready to deliver pizza   on the heels of the madman who
steps on the musical scale   a flash of sunlight—I stop writing
the little trail of the zipper exposes the back of night   waiting to
be whipped by the Master of Memory   the emperor stamps
the imperial jade seal at the end of the long scroll of mountains
and rivers

nebular ink dots on rice paper—in accord with the cosmos   paint-
ing pictures makes me euphoric   ink dots cluster disperse
depending on the flow of random scattering   forest beyond the
borders of language   *good fortune depends on disaster / disaster
conceals good fortune*   I am aimless freedom   listening
closely to the whispers of snowflakes guarding the vortex of day
and night at the center of the mysterious river

從香港到南寧跨過病的國境　　　我被祖先們的
手號脈　　　包括南陽的張仲景　　　*經方者*
本草石之寒溫　　　量疾病之淺深　　　我側臥成山
脈　　　追趕平原的燈火馬蹄　　　針與灸相輔相
成　　　九顆星球在道的魔術師的手中轉動　　　辯
證才是病的真理

回頭是岸　　　永不停止的浪花正如輓歌　　　用
經絡充電　　　　向黃昏的祖父和月亮的盈虧學
習 ── 我和死神對弈　　　黎明從火車站出發
滿載語言的緩衝器嘎嘎作響　　　陽氣從山谷中
悄悄升起　　　遺忘的森林勒住了風

群山和海浪　　　進入夢中危險的歷程　　　地
下的樹根在爭論　　　多汁的石榴爆炸　　　毒
蘑菇指責讚美的天空　　　　大師用琴弦撥動亂
世　　　壞念頭的蒼蠅在頭上盤旋　　　我打坐

crossing the national borders of illness from Hong Kong to Nan-
ning   the hands of the ancestors feel my pulse   including
Zhang Zhongjing of Nanyang   *physician's prescription   book
of healing herbs and stone needles for cold and warmth   measure
the depths of the sickness*   I lie on my side becoming a mountain
range   chase the flame-bright hooves of the horses on the plains
needle and moxa each complement the other   the nine planets
rotate in the hands of the magician of the Da   dialectics is really
the truth of illness

turning back to the shore   the ceaseless spindrift like an elegiac
song   recharge through the meridians   learn from the grand-
father of dusk and the moon's waxing and waning—I play chess
with the god of death   dawn embarks from the train station
the buffer overloaded with language grinds and screeches   yang
qi-energy rises with a murmur from the ravine   the forgotten
forest has reined in the wind

mountain chains and ocean waves   enter the dangerous jour-
ney of the dream   tree roots argue underground   juicy
pomegranates explode   poisonous mushrooms denounce
praises to heaven   the master uses the strings of the qin to
pluck the turbulent world   as the flies of wicked thoughts
spiral overhead   I sit in meditation

第三十四章

關於香港　　我一無所知
帶上地下之書去旅行
飛機降落　　珊瑚礁閃爍
陌生人找燈的坐標
天際線的敍事推向性高潮
青蛙在內臟中跳躍

渡船　　過渡中的過渡
沒有聽眾　　詩人們互相傾聽
我和商禽一起吃夜宵
在水蒸氣的玻璃上畫小人
呼吸的午夜在腳下

從北加州小鎮搬到香港，
用右手緊緊抓住左手
當厄運騎着幸運兒的馬
算命先生　　從羅盤指向未來
幼兒園大門被塗成彩虹

首屆香港國際詩歌之夜
在革命和宗教之間
詩歌是另一種聲音
發酒瘋的颱風失去靈魂
叮叮車　　憂傷的軌道
上環棺材店　　太陽砸門

六四晚會是新的黑名單
而活着的都是守夜人
燭火呼應　　正是缺席的意義
死亡的棋路沒有規則
無路可逃　　被獵殺的字眼

XXXIV.

about Hong Kong   I know nothing
carrying an underground book for the trip
land at Kai Tak Airport   coral reef shimmers
strangers look for the coordinates of lights
the skyline's narrative pushes toward climax
frogs hop inside the gut

ferryboat   "Transition in Transition" Poetry Festival
no audience   poets listen to each other in rapt attention
Shang Qin and I   eat a late-night meal together
draw little figures on the fogged windows
midnight breathes beneath our feet

from a small town in Northern California to the Fragrant Harbour
take the right hand and tightly grip the left
when misfortune rides the horse of good fortune
fortune teller   geomantic compass points to the future
kindergarten school gate painted in rainbows

first gathering of the International Poetry Nights
between revolution and religion   *poetry is the other voice*
the insanely drunk typhoon loses its soul
dingding tram   sorrowful tracks
Sheung Wan coffin shops   sun smashes the doors

June Fourth vigils are the new blacklist
and the living are all guardians of the night
candle flames echo   the meaning of absence
the chess moves of death have no rules
no way to flee   words hunted and killed

警笛沸點　火光　剪影
如水　大街小巷　洪流　壩
防毒面具　旗幟呼喊　兄弟
爬山　花流血　時代的斜坡

喂　手機屏幕的笑臉
暴風雨穿上官方的制服
只可惜你戴起了口罩
聽不清楚是不是你在說話
九聲調的粵語不再陌生
哼着黃昏的無言歌

網 —— 人類是魚的祖先
正進入大數據的生活
手被牽動　心在右舵
自由不過是驗證我的名字
當病毒和數字王國為鄰

野獸們悄悄進入城市
用水泥鑄造成金幣
奴隸們扛着歷史的樓梯
螺旋的邏輯可進可退
戰爭與瘟疫　大海
是生銹水龍頭的眼淚

香港不是我旅程的終點
在語言流變的激流中
審查官用筆勾掉新的現實
我被香港收留　填海蓋樓
前往天堂的火車站

窗口面對海灣的全景
大歷史升級到單人牢房
夢中的鳥飛過　短暫而永久

boiling point of police sirens   flames   paper-cut silhouettes
like water   high streets and back alleys   flood currents   dams
gas masks   roar of flags   brothers
climb a mountain   flowers bleed   slope of the times

hello   cellphone screen's smiley face
the rainstorm has put on an official uniform
it's too bad you're wearing a mask
can't hear if you're really sayin' anything
nine tones of Cantonese no longer unfamiliar
humming the silent song of dusk

net—humans are the ancestors of fish
now entering a life of big data
pulled by the hands   heart at the right rudder
freedom nothing more than the verification of my name
when viruses and digital domains become neighbors

wild beasts steal stealthily into the city
use cement to cast gold coins
slaves carry the staircase of history on their backs
spiral logic can advance or retreat
war and pandemic   the ocean
the tears of a rusty faucet

Hong Kong isn't the end of my journey
in the shifting currents of language
censors use a pen to cross out new realities
Hong Kong has taken me in   reclaiming land from the sea
to build more towers   the train station
on the way to paradise

window faces a panoramic view of the bay
Big History upgrades to a solitary prison cell
birds fly by in a dream   ephemeral and everlasting

我是你　　歧路的陌生人
等待收割光芒的季節
送信　　明天卻沒有地址

I am you   a stranger on the sidetracks
waiting for the season to harvest blades of light
sending letters   though tomorrow has no address

AFTERWORD

Already the end of the year and yet this place feels like spring, a sunlight brilliance. I picked up my pen in the summer of 2010; since completing the final word, the eleven years that this writing demanded, from start to finish, should be considered a promise to myself. Through the catastrophe of suffering a debilitating stroke and the language impediments that followed, the manuscript had to be shelved; I started to draw and paint to pass the time. Three years later I started to write again, stumbling along, wobbling like a rusty pendulum, searching for that innate, inner compulsion.

The days are filled with unexpected winds and clouds, storms to weather, a pandemic that has altered the course of humanity, quarantine becoming the normal state all over the world. I'm trapped in Hong Kong, can hardly step foot outside the door. One could say that fortune can be found in misfortune, a chance to throw all my energy and focus into writing.

I remember twenty years ago walking with Li Tuo at the Berkeley Pier. The morning mist was thick that day and a fog-bell rang out. I said, "Fog-bell, that's a nice word—could be borrowed for a poem." Li Tuo nodded and replied, "You should write a long poem, something with a sense of history."

In the summer of 2007, after moving from the US to Hong Kong, so many years of living in exile finally turned into a relatively stable situation. Looking back, post-1989 in particular, besides scattered bits here and there written for articles and essays, most of that period I hadn't wholly examined or reimagined, and so it felt like the right time to start this long poem.

During the surging pandemic, I became more conscious of time's urgency—that what encompasses life and energy, along with the creative faculties, could be cut short or recede at any moment, in accordance with the Buddhist concept of *anitya* ("impermanence").

One significant thing to note: in order to unify style and form, the development of the whole poem had to be altered; above all, the first ten sections required heavy revision, some sections were completely rewritten. Most of the poems in their original form were published in *Today* magazine and can be referenced there. My gratitude and thanks to friends and family who accompanied me through my difficulties; thanks to Jin Siyan, Chen Lichuan, and Tian Yuan—"ideal readers" who helped me tune my instrument; and a special thanks to Lam To Kwan, who published this book during difficult times.

—BEI DAO
APRIL 2022

NOTES

page

POEM III

15 *"no one was killed on the square"*: As reported by official Chinese state media.

from West Berlin to Beijing: Bei Dao lived in West Berlin from May to September 1989 as a fellow of the DAAD (German Academic Exchange Service) Artists-in-Berlin Program. It was the first foreign city he ever visited.

17 *scanned photos transmitted*: Because of restrictive government regulation of CNN in Beijing, only scanned news photos could be sent to the Hong Kong office over the telephone lines.

POEM IV

21 *Güntzelstrasse 50*: The address in West Berlin where Bei Dao lived for four months in 1989.

symphony Pathétique: The Russian composer Pyotr Ilyich Tchaikovsky's Symphony no. 6 in B Minor, op. 74—his last complete symphony.

Kubin: Wolfgang Kubin (b. 1945), German sinologist, translator, and writer.

23 *Shao Fei*: (b. 1954), contemporary Chinese painter and Bei Dao's first wife, with whom he has a daughter, Tiantian (Zhao Tianji).

the open letter signed: Bei Dao initiated a joint open letter to the government signed by thirty-three intellectuals on February 16, 1989.

POEM VI

29 *Kringsjå Student Village*: Housing area at the University of Oslo where Bei Dao was a visiting scholar from September to December 1989.

Maiping: Chen Maiping (b. 1952), Chinese writer and translator who moved to Sweden in 1990.

"Solveig's Song": Song from the second orchestral suite of the Norwegian composer Edvard Grieg's *Peer Gynt*, op. 23.

Harald's family: Harald Bøckman (b. 1945), Norwegian sinologist.

31 *Duo Duo*: (b. 1951), Chinese poet and short-story writer.

Bonnie M.: Bonnie S. McDougall (b. 1941), Australian sinologist and translator. She was the first to translate Bei Dao's work into English.

resolve to resume Today: The decision to resume publication of *Jintian* (Today) in Sweden was made in the Oslo airport. The groundbreaking literary journal was originally cofounded by Bei Dao and Mang Ke in Beijing in 1978 and continues to today.

POEM VII

33 *Zhao Yifan's hands*: Zhao Yifan (1935–1988) collected a massive library of underground writings and publications through the Cultural Revolution. He had a disability since childhood.

yellow cover books: A series of nearly one hundred canonical books of modernist Western literature published between 1961 and 1966 "for internal distribution" among high-level cadre circles.

"The East Is Red": One of the most famous revolutionary songs in China.

9/13 Lin Biao Incident: Lin Biao (1907–1971), the Chinese politician and Marshal of the People's Republic of China who died in a suspicious plane crash in Outer Mongolia on September 13, 1971, after allegedly conspiring to assassinate Chairman Mao.

Waves: The first draft of Bei Dao's novella *Waves* (波動, *bodong*) was finished in November 1974 in a darkroom.

35 *Pure Brightness Festival*: A nationwide protest movement that spread around the time of the Pure Brightness Festival (Qingming Festival) in 1976.

Yan Li: (b. 1954), Chinese poet and painter.

Mang Ke: (b. 1951), Chinese poet and painter; cofounder of the literary journal *Today*.

This is the safest place in Beijing: What Zhao Yifan said when Bei Dao passed him the manuscript of *Waves*. Bei Dao picked up the manuscript from him two days later; two months after that, Zhao Yifan was imprisoned.

Yifan released from prison: Zhao Yifan was released from prison on December 23, 1976. He could no longer use his legs to walk.

my tears flowed and overflowed . . . : Lines from a poem by the Russian poet Nikolay Nekrasov (1821–1878).

POEM VIII

Lines in italics throughout this poem are from book 2 ("To Govern") of the *Analects* (論語, *lun yu*), a collection of sayings by Confucius compiled by his disciples in the centuries after his death in 479 BCE.

39 *that stray dog mourning his lost home*: In Sima Qian's *Records of the Grand Historian* (太史公書, *taishigong shu*) there is an anecdote about someone seeing Confucius standing at the east city gate and describing him to Zigong, a disciple of Confucius, as having an odd appearance and "crestfallen like a homeless wandering dog."

POEM IX

41 *it is now time for stone to bloom*: See Paul Celan's poem "Corona."

POEM X

45 *two clocks run out of sync . . .* : See Franz Kafka's diary entry for January 16, 1922.

Kafka the jackdaw: The name Kafka comes from the Czech word *kavka*, meaning "jackdaw."

Josephine the singer's: The last short story Kafka wrote before his death was "Josefine, die Sängerin oder Das Volk der Mäuse" ("Josephine the Singer, or the Mouse Folk").

47 *"At the Construction of the Great Wall of China"*: Allusion to Kafka's posthumously published story "Beim Bau der Chinesischen Mauer."

City of the Sun: Allusion to Tommaso Campanella's philosophical work *Civitas solis* (1602).

Revolver Revue: Czech literary journal first published in the form of samizdat in 1985.

sends an invitation . . .: *Revolver Revue* invited the editors and friends of *Today* to a conference in Prague in May 1993.

POEM XI

49 *better to forget each other . . .*: From the *Zhuangzi* (莊子, late fourth century BCE), chapter 6, "The Great and Venerable Teacher" (大宗師, *dazongshi*).

Today marked "The Moment" forever: The words "The Moment" appeared in English on the cover of the inaugural issue of the underground literary magazine *Today* in December 1978.

Li Tuo: (b. 1939), Chinese literary critic.

51 *Gao Xingjian*: (b. 1940), Chinese novelist and playwright. He won the Nobel Prize in Literature in 2000.

looking left then right words digress: An idiom from *Mencius*, "King Hui of Liang II," that means to try to change the subject of a conversation.

Old Wood: Lao Mu (1963–2020), Chinese poet who was an exile in France and for a period lived homeless on the streets in Paris.

55 *I am a concrete worker I am a blacksmith*: Bei Dao worked in construction for eleven years, from 1969 to 1980: six years as a concrete worker and five years as a blacksmith.

my sister Shan Shan's drowned spirit: Zhao Shanshan (1953–1976), Bei Dao's sister who drowned while saving someone near the city of Xiangyang in Hubei province.

at last history has given us a chance: The first sentence of the foreword in the inaugural issue of *Today* magazine.

57 *Rudin's tears*: *Rudin* was the first novel written by the Russian writer Ivan Turgenev, originally published in 1856.

Bright Horse River: Liangma River in Beijing.

59 *Poul Borum, my judge*: (1934–1996), Danish writer, poet, editor, and critic. Borum wrote a positive review of Bei Dao's collection *Old Snow* (舊雪, *jiuxue*) in a Danish newspaper in 1991. In his collection of essays *Midnight's Gate*, Bei Dao says that Borum wrote a newspaper column about poetry that was commonly referred to as "Borum's Court."

61 *Tomas Tranströmer*: (1931–2015), Swedish poet, psychologist, and translator. He won the Nobel Prize in Literature in 2011.

63 *four/nine city gates*: The four gates of the inner city and the nine gates of the imperial city in Beijing.

One Hundred Flowers Hidden Deep: Name of a hutong street in Beijing.

the new subject is class struggle: In 1962, Mao Zedong proclaimed, "Never forget the class struggle."

67 *from Chongqing to Fengjie*: The Tang dynasty poet Du Fu (712–770) lived in Kuizhou, modern-day Fengjie County in Sichuan province, for one year and ten months (766–768).

the young men of the gorge make light of death: From Du Fu's poem "The Most Skillful"(最能行, *zuinengxing*).

Li Bai . . . Gao Shi: Tang dynasty poets and contemporaries of Du Fu—Li Bai over ten years older than Du Fu and Gao Shi roughly eight years older.

a smooth lake rises in the towering gorge: From Mao Zedong's poem "Prelude to Water Melody: Swimming."

69 *sough sough no end . . . Great River rolls in*: From Du Fu's poem "Climbing to a Height" (登高, *denggao*), written on the Double Ninth Festival in 767.

balanced between heaven and earth: From Du Fu's poem "Thoughts Written While Traveling at Night" (旅夜書懷, *lüyeshuhuai*).

POEM XVI

71 *Balmont*: Konstantin Balmont (1867–1942), Russian symbolist poet and translator.

73 *savors the almonds of Mother*: The poet Paul Celan associated almonds with the memory of his mother, who used them in baking bread and cakes when he was a child.

Breytenbach: Breyten Breytenbach (b. 1939), South African writer, poet, and painter who wrote the memoir *The True Confessions of an Albino Terrorist* (1984).

Darwish: Mahmoud Darwish (1941–2008), Palestinian poet who wrote the poetry collection *A Lover from Palestine* (1966) as well as a poem with the same title.

Adonis: Pen name of the Syrian poet Ali Ahmad Said Esber (b. 1930).

POEM XVII

75 *of autumn . . . prongs my heart*: From the poem "Chansons d'Automne" by Paul Verlaine (1844–1896). Lines from the poem were broadcast by the BBC to signal to the French Resistance the beginning of D-Day and the landing of Allied troops at Normandy on June 6, 1944.

POEM XVIII

79 *reality sandwich*: See Allen Ginsberg's *Reality Sandwiches* (1963).

Tyger! Tyger!: Translation of the Chinese translation of William Blake's "The Tyger."

our hearts . . . our own seed: Translation of the Chinese translation of Allen Ginsberg's "Sunflower Sutra."

POEM XIX

83 *from the public squares . . . romance can be found*: From the editor's note in the Chinese edition of a selection of Federico García Lorca's poems (洛爾迦詩鈔, *Luoerjia shichao*) published in 1956, translated by Dai Wangshu and edited by Shi Jincun.

85 *Residencia de Estudiantes*: The cultural and educational center of arts and science founded in Madrid in 1910 that complemented university education. Lorca, Salvador Dalí, Luis Buñuel, Severo Ochoa, and Manuel de Falla were residents there among many others.

Laura García: Laura García-Lorca de los Ríos (b. 1953), director of the Huerta de San Vicente in Granada, a museum dedicated to Lorca, and president of the Federico García Lorca Foundation.

Paul Jean-Ortiz: (1957–2014), French sinologist and diplomat.

POEM XX

87 *how slow life moves / how violent hope proves*: Translation of the Chinese translation of Guillaume Apollinaire's "Le pont Mirabeau."

ALICE: Acronym for the post-Tiananmen Massacre organization in France *L'Association de liaison avec les intellectuels chinois en exil*.

Operation Yellowbird: 黃雀行動 (*huangque xingdong*), also translated as Operation Siskin. An underground network organized after the Tiananmen Massacre to help Chinese dissidents escape from Hong Kong to France.

Lü Min: Marianne Bujard (b. 1958), Swiss sinologist and main director of ALICE.

7 rue de Venise: Bei Dao lived in a studio at this address near the Centre Pompidou for a year and three months from 1999 to 2000.

Gao Yuan: (b. 1950), Chinese photographer who has lived in exile in Paris since 1990.

89 *Lao Mu*: See note for "Old Wood" in Poem XI.

Song Lin: (b. 1959), Chinese poet and one of the poetry editors for *Today*.

POEM XXI

91 *Dr. Li Wenliang*: (1986–2020), Chinese Manchurian ophthalmologist and whistleblower. Dr. Li issued the first warning about cases of a new SARS-like virus in Wuhan in December 2019. He was silenced by authorities and died from COVID-19 on February 7, 2020, less than a month after being infected.

the truth is more important than vindication: From an interview with Dr. Li Wenliang published in *Caijing* (財經) magazine published on January 30, 2020.

101 *photographed from a high angle*: Photographed by Mu Xiaocheng, who used to teach in the photography department at the Beijing Film Academy. He witnessed the scene from the departure area with various senior military officers—Bei Dao being escorted to his plane by thirty to forty soldiers of the Armed Police Force.

POEM XXIV

103 *open the second page of the new century*: The Palestinian poet Mahmoud Darwish invited a special delegation from the International Parliament of Writers to visit the Occupied Palestinian Territories in the spring of 2002. The delegation included Bei Dao, Russell Banks, Breyten Breytenbach, Vincenzo Consolo, Juan Goytisolo, Christian Salmon, José Saramago, and Wole Soyinka.

105 *he uses the heart to make a fist*: Mahmoud Darwish died on August 9, 2008, in Houston, Texas, due to complications from heart surgery.

POEM XXV

107 *Reference News*: (参考消息, *Cankao xiaoxi*), the official People's Republic of China digest of the world press that started in 1931.

109 *the Pacific Ocean pounds on the captain's coffin*: Allusion to Pablo Neruda's book *Los versos del capitán* (*The Captain's Verses*) (1952). After his death on September 23, 1973, Neruda was buried in the Cementerio General de Santiago; in 1992 his remains were exhumed and reburied at his house on Isla Negra, a coastal area in Chile along the Pacific Ocean.

POEM XXVI

113 *by the sea's side hear the dark-vowelled birds*: From Dylan Thomas's poem "Especially when the October wind."

riding the noon train out to Long Island: Bei Dao taught a poetry class at SUNY Stony Brook in the spring of 2000.

115 *C. N. Yang*: Chen-Ning Yang (b. 1922), theoretical physicist who won the Nobel Prize in Physics in 1957.

symposium for Chinese writers in exile: Organized by the PEN American Center in October 1989.

I pursue someone . . . No one: Translated from the Chinese translation of Octavio Paz's poem "La calle" ("The Street").

China Independent Film Festival: Organized by Columbia University, Lincoln Center, *Today* magazine, and others in May 2007.

two women survivors stagger . . . : See the 2002 documentary film *The Weather Underground.*

you don't need a weatherman . . .: From Bob Dylan's song "Subterranean Homesick Blues."

POEM XXVII

119 *Gennady Aygi*: (1934–2006), Chuvash poet, essayist, and translator.

Rotterdam sky: The Poetry International Festival Rotterdam is held every June. Aygi was a special guest of the festival in 1992. Several poets participated in a translation workshop to translate Aygi's poetry into other languages.

Zhang Zao: (1962–2010), Chinese poet who left China in 1986 and for many years was the poetry editor for *Today*. He received a doctorate in literature in Germany and lived there until his death from lung cancer.

each word . . . a tyrant: From an interview Zhang Zao conducted with Aygi published in *Today* (no. 3, 1992).

Judge Borum: See note for "Poem XIII."

only a kind of silver . . . on the shoulders: Translation of the Chinese translation of Aygi's poem "Alongside the Forest" (see *Field-Russia*, translated from the Russian by Peter France [New Directions, 2007]).

Gu Cheng: (1956–1993), pioneering poet, essayist, and novelist who moved to Waiheke Island in New Zealand in 1987.

121 *Beloit Poetry Festival*: Bei Dao taught at Beloit College for seven weeks of the year from 1999 to 2006. In the fall of 2003, he helped to organize the poetry festival with other colleagues.

that forest . . . of the ax: From Bei Dao's poem "Salute—To Aygi" (致敬—給G. 艾基, *shijing—gei G. Aiji*).

POEM XXVIII

123 *I've returned*: Bei Dao returned to Beijing for the first time in thirteen years on December 2, 2001.

city gate city gate how high how tall: From a Beijing nursery rhyme. See Bei Dao's autobiography, *City Gate, Open Up* (New Directions, 2017).

secret base . . . music conservatory: The China Conservatory of Music used to be located at 17 Qianhai West Street, next to the secret residence where Bei Dao was put up.

Yan Wenjing: (1915–2005), Chinese writer.

Niu Han: (1923–2013), Chinese poet.

Cai Qijiao: (1918–2007), Chinese poet and translator.

Feng Yidai: (1913–2005), Chinese writer, editor, and translator.

Fred Wakeman: Frederic Wakeman (1937–2006), American scholar of East Asian history.

125 *Huang Rui*: (b. 1952), Chinese artist.

POEM XXIX

127 *spring of 2005*: Bei Dao was a writer-in-residence at the University of Alabama at Tuscaloosa from January to May 2005.

129 *the king's stone didn't hit me*: See Bei Dao's poem "Purple" (紫色, *zise*) in *Landscape Over Zero* (零度以上的风景, *lingdu yishang de fengjing*) published in 1996 and reissued in 2001 in the collection *At the Sky's Edge: Poems 1991–1996*: "someone on the throne / throws a stone // doesn't hit me" (有人從王位上 / 扔出石頭 // 沒有擊中我).

winter of 2006: From 2005 to 2007 Bei Dao taught a poetry class in the spring semester at the University of Notre Dame.

summer of 1994: Bei Dao was a writer-in-residence at the University of Michigan from the spring of 1994 to the summer of 1995.

POEM XXX

131 *anti-spiritual pollution campaign*: A failed political campaign launched in October 1983 under paramount leader Deng Xiaoping to eliminate both leftists and decadent rightists in the Communist Party by taking active measures against cultural and ideological bourgeois liberalism. Bei Dao was an outspoken critic of the campaign, which was quietly canceled by the end of January 1984.

"comrades fight for you . . .": Bei Dao quotes Gary Snyder.

133 *form is emptiness . . .*: From the *Mahaprajna Paramita Heart Sutra*.

Hong Kong island to the poetry festival: The International Poetry Nights in Hong Kong, a poetry festival spearheaded by Bei Dao, held its first gathering in November 2009.

three of us cross the border: A conversation between Bei Dao, Gary Snyder, and Eliot Weinberger that was later published in a book through the Poetry Nights festival titled *Ancient Enmity* (古老的敵意, *gulao de diyi*, 2012).

135 *He cries out . . . three times!*: From Gary Snyder's poem "Meeting the Mountains."

137 *Adachi Souichi*: (安達壯一, Anda Zhuangyi, b. 1950), former executive at Sony (China).

twentieth anniversary of Today magazine: Celebrated in Tokyo in early December 1998.

"seas of the millennium": Theme of the second international poetry festival held in Shizuoka, Japan, in November 2000.

139 *Shun Korenaga*: (是永駿, Shi Yong Jun, b. 1943), scholar, poet, and translator.

Izu has no dancing girl: Allusion to Yasunari Kawabata's novel *The Dancing Girl of Izu* (1926).

poetry monument: Bei Dao's stone poetry monument in Kamogawa, Japan, was unveiled on November 19, 2016.

Tanikawa Shuntaro: (b. 1931), Japanese poet and translator. His first collection of poetry, *Two Billion Light Years of Loneliness*, was published in 1952.

141 *"a conversation between two Eastern civilizations"*: *Today* magazine and the online journal *Almost Island* cohost the India-China Writers' Dialogue series. The quote is by the political psychologist, social theorist, and critic Ashis Nandy from his opening remarks at the first conference, held in February 2009 in New Delhi.

I. Allan Sealy: (b. 1951), Indian novelist.

Magris: Claudio Magris (b. 1939), Italian scholar, translator, and novelist.

143 *Ouyang Jianghe*: (b. 1956), Chinese poet and critic.

Blue City: Jodhpur, a city in the Thar Desert in the state of Rajasthan famous for its blue-painted buildings.

fourth round of conversations: The fourth conference of the India-China Writers' Dialogue series took place in Hong Kong and Hangzhou in October 2018.

Tagore: Rabindranath Tagore (1861–1941), Bengali poet, writer, painter, and composer who in 1913 became the first non-European to win the Nobel Prize in Literature.

145 *abducted by the translucent devilfish*: Around noon on April 8, 2012, Bei Dao was preparing to go out on a boat with his wife and son, Gan Qi and Do Do, at Wu Kai Sha Beach in Hong Kong when he had a stroke.

good fortune depends on disaster . . .: From the *Daodejing* (道德經, ca. 400 BCE), chapter 58.

147 *Zhang Zhongjing*: (150–219 CE), physician and medical scientist of the Eastern Han who wrote the landmark work *Treatise on Cold Pathogenic and Miscellaneous Diseases* (傷寒雜病論, *shanghanzabinglun*).

physician's prescription . . . sickness: From the *History of the Former Han Dynasty* (前漢書, *qianhanshu*, ca. 111 CE), in the chapter "Art and Literature" (藝文志, *yiwenzhi*).

149 *underground book*: Refers to Bei Dao's novella *Waves* (波動, *bodong*), published by the Chinese University of Hong Kong Press in 1988. See notes for "Poem VII."

"Transition in Transition" Poetry Festival: The theme of the first Hong Kong International Poetry Festival, held in January 1997.

Shang Qin: (1930–2010), Chinese poet who moved to Taiwan in 1948.

from a small town . . . to the Fragrant Harbour: In the fall of 2007, Bei Dao moved from Davis, California, to accept a teaching position at the Chinese University of Hong Kong.

between revolution . . . the other voice: From Octavio Paz's essay "La otra voz" in his book *La otra voz: Poesía y fin de siglo* (*The Other Voice: Poetry and the End of the Century*, 1990). "The other voice" was also the theme of the inaugural International Poetry Nights in Hong Kong festival in 2009. See note for "Poem XXX."

151 *it's too bad . . . really sayin' anything*: From the poem "Cityscape" (城市風景, *chengshi fengjing*) by Yesi (也斯, 1949–2013), pen name of the Hong Kong poet, writer, and translator Leung Ping-kwan.

net . . . life of big data: See Bei Dao's poem "Notes from the City of the Sun" (太陽城札記, *taiyangcheng zhaji*), written in 1973. The last section of the poem reads: 「生活：網」 ("Life: a Net").

ACKNOWLEDGMENTS

Thanks to Srikanth Reddy, Emily Stokes, Amanda Gersten, and the rest of the staff at the *Paris Review*, and to Sharmistha Mohanty et al. at *Almost Island*, for first publishing some of these translations.

Thanks to Jon Beacham at The Brother In Elysium for publishing "Prologue" as a two-color letterpress broadside as part of his subscription program.

Thanks to Lucas Klein and Eliot Weinberger for their detailed feedback on a draft of this translation.

Thanks to Barbara Epler for her virtuoso fine-tuning, to Ryan Nichols for his assiduous proofreading, and to Lam To Kwan for proofing the Chinese.

Thanks to Joan Wong for the beautiful cover design and to Eileen Bellamy for the beautiful interior design.

Thanks to the Omina Freundeshilfe Foundation for a grant that supported this translation.

Thanks to Bei Dao for entrusting me with his poem and for putting up with my questions. All slips and inaccuracies by the translator will be resolved in the next life.

BEI DAO, pen name of Zhao Zhenkai, was born in Beijing in 1949. Hailed as "the soul of post-Mao poetry" (Yunte Huang) and praised for his "intense lyricism" (Pankaj Mishra), Bei Dao is one of contemporary China's most distinguished poets and the cofounder of the landmark underground literary journal *Jintian* (Today). He has received numerous international awards for his work, including the Cikada Prize in Sweden, the Golden Wreath Award in Macedonia, the Aragana Poetry Prize in Morocco, the Jeanette Schocken Literary Prize in Germany, the PEN/Barbara Goldsmith Freedom to Write Award, and the 2nd Yakamochi Medal in Japan; he is also an honorary member of the American Academy of Arts and Letters. Since 2007 he has been the Professor of Humanities at the Chinese University of Hong Kong, and currently resides between Hong Kong and Beijing. He acquired U.S. citizenship in 2009. New Directions publishes ten of his books, most recently his autobiography *City Gate, Open Up*. Bei Dao's poetry has been translated into over thirty languages.

JEFFREY YANG is the author of the poetry books *Line and Light*; *Hey, Marfa*; *Vanishing-Line*; and *An Aquarium*. He is the translator of Bei Dao's autobiography *City Gate, Open Up*; Nobel Peace Prize Laureate Liu Xiaobo's *June Fourth Elegies*; Ahmatjan Osman's *Uyghurland, the Farthest Exile*; Su Shi's *East Slope*; and an anthology of classical Chinese poems, *Rhythm 226*. He is the editor at large at New Directions Publishing.